Discover the Cotswolds

town and country walks

Published by Sigma Leisure - an imprint of Sigma Press, Stobart House, Pontyclerc, Penybanc Road, Ammanford, Carmarthenshire SA18 3HP.

British Library Cataloguing in Publication Data
A CIP record for this book is available from the British Library.

ISBN: 978-1-85058--967-9

Typesetting and Design by: Sigma Press, Ammanford, Carmarthenshire

Cover photographs: ©Gordon Whiting

Photographs: ©Gordon Whiting

Maps: Rebecca Terry

Printed by: TJ International Ltd, Padstow, Cornwall

Discover the Cotswolds

town and country walks

Roy Woodcock

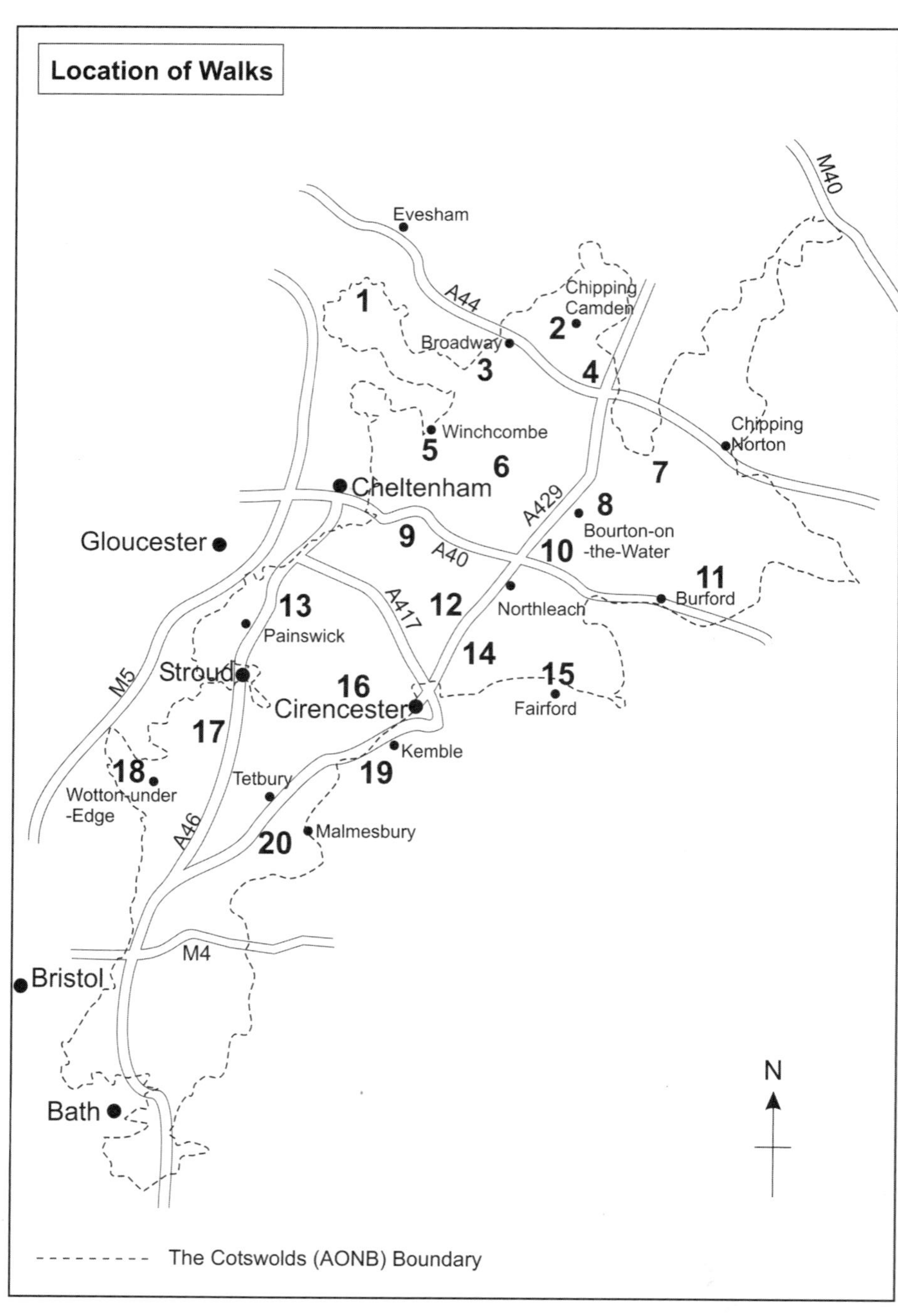
Location of Walks
M40
Evesham
A44
1
Chipping
Camden
2
Broadway
3
4
Winchcombe
5
6
Chipping
Norton
7
Cheltenham
A429
8
Gloucester
9
A40
Bourton-on
-the-Water
10
11
Northleach
Burford
A417
12
13
Painswick
14
15
Stroud
M5
16
Cirencester
Fairford
17
Kemble
19
18
Tetbury
Wotton-under
-Edge
A46
Malmesbury
20
M4
Bristol
Bath
N
The Cotswolds (AONB) Boundary

Contents

Introduction

Extent

Although difficult to define precisely, the Cotswolds are generally considered to extend from Bath in the south to near Banbury in the north, and from Cheltenham in the west to Witney and Woodstock in the east. They are limestone hills which form a *cuesta*, that is a hill with one side which is steep, the escarpment, and the other side which is more gentle, the dip. West of the escarpment are isolated hills such as Bredon, Cam Long Down and Robin's Wood Hill, which are outliers, remnants of the time when the Cotswolds extended much further west than at present.

Jurassic

The Cotswolds consist of different layers of limestone, all belonging to the Jurassic period, the geological period named after the Jura Mountains on the France-Switzerland border. This period dates from 206 to 144 million years ago, and at that time what is now England was somewhere in the region of the Mediterranean. The North American continent and Europe were beginning to drift apart and a large sea opened up between Africa and Europe. This enlarged Mediterranean Sea was known as Tethys Ocean and was a large expanse of shallow, warm sea, rich in animal life. As these animals died and fell to the sea bed, huge deposits of rock were accumulating, and when compressed and uplifted gave rise to large areas of limestone. These include the Jurassic limestones which have created the Cotswolds. These rocks are rich in fossils, notably ammonites, belemnites and gryphaea, as the warm shallow seas were teeming with life. On land it was the time of the dinosaurs.

The Jurassic period is divided into Lower, Middle and Upper. The Lower, the oldest, is called the Lias with outcrops in Gloucestershire and elsewhere to the west of the Cotswold escarpment. Younger rocks make up the Middle Jurassic, the main Cotswolds rocks and to the east of these are the Upper and youngest of the Jurassic rocks outcropping near Oxford.

Jurassic rocks extend from the North Yorkshire coast across England to the Dorset coast. Many of these are limestones laid down on the sea bed and consist of remains of dead sea creatures. In places and at certain times there was mud and clay eroded from neighbouring land also being deposited on the sea bed to create clays and marls as well as the limestone. And in places too there were deposits of sand which formed other sedimentary rocks. So there is a variety of sedimentary rocks being laid down in the Jurassic period but the Cotswold area is the main region for limestones. Some of these are called oolitic because of the small circular, egg-like fragments which form this rock. Others are shelly and contain many fragments of dead sea creatures. Different animals in different locations means that there are many different limestones.

In places where the deposits of limestone have been fairly uniform, thick beds of rock have been created. These are very good for building and are known as freestones, as they can be quarried and cut in any direction to make large blocks. These blocks, seen in many Cotswold buildings are called ashlar. In other places the rock breaks into thinner pieces and may be seen in some of the stone walls, and in many places are used as a roofing stone.

Geology and Landscape

A series of earth movements heaved up the limestone and tilted it, so that the western margin creates the steep slope known as the Cotswolds scarp, best seen at Birdlip Hill above Cheltenham and Fish Hill above Broadway. On the top of the scarp where the gentle east facing dip slope resembles a plateau, eastward flowing streams have cut valleys in which nestle many farms and most of the villages. Stow-on-the-Wold and Chipping Norton are exceptions to this generalisation. Many of the valleys are dry because the rock is permeable and the water quickly drains away underground.

Much of the dip slope is open wold, where the huge sheep runs of the Middle Ages were located. Broad, rolling countryside extends from Chipping Campden and Winchcombe towards the east. Further south near Cheltenham and Stroud the landscape is broken up by deep valleys, but east of these towards Bibury and Burford, the undulating wold scenery is to be found again.

The dip slope is crossed by the Thames and its tributaries the Evenlode, Windrush, Churn and Coln, which often cut deep valleys. Comments about the source of the Thames can be seen in Walks 9 and 19.

The main rivers flowing west are the Frome and Bristol Avon, although the Avon has a lengthy route, flowing east at first and then south before heading westwards.

The name of Cotswolds is possibly derived from *cot*, the Saxon word for a sheep enclosure, which would be quite appropriate, but it may also have been derived from the name of a person, Cod, a Saxon leader in this area. The *wold* part either means high ground, or it may be the same as *wald*, meaning forest.

The Cotswold region had been inhabited for a long time before Cod, and evidence of Stone Age settlements can be seen in the numerous barrows, some of which show the use of dry stone walling nearly 5000 years ago. Roman remains can be seen in many places, notably at Chedworth (See Walk 12) and Witcombe (Walk 9), showing that they too, settled here, and in Saxon times the area was still important. Gloucester was a major town in England, and perhaps would have been the capital city if the Normans had not arrived and shifted the centre of influence to the south east.

Visitors to the Cotswolds increased after William Morris and his Pre-Raphaelite friends came to visit in the 1870s and were full of praise for the scenery. CR Ashbee and the Guild of Handicrafts moved to Chipping Campden in 1902 and many other craftsmen came into this delightful rural area, to Broadway, Sapperton and elsewhere (see Walks 2 and 16). The popularity of the area has continued to increase up to the present day, when the landscape still attracts visitors in large numbers as well as attracting many well-to-do people to come and live here.

Land Use

The thin alkaline soils were traditionally used as pasture, growing grass to feed sheep. It was their wool which made landowners wealthy in former centuries. The wool towns such as Stroud, Witney, Bradford-on-Avon and others still retain some old mills, though now largely converted to other uses. An even more impressive reminder of the wealth brought in by wool are the magnificent churches. Wealthy merchants not only built magnificent houses but also financed the building of churches, because of their desire to have a church as grand as that in the neighbouring village.

Water power was used in the woollen industry and the larger streams and deeper valleys were particularly suitable, notably at Stroud. By the end of the 18th century the woollen industry was declining as competition was growing, especially from Yorkshire where ample coal was available for steam power.

Crop growing was not very important in the past, but the need to produce home grown food, especially during World War II, brought the discovery that the thin alkaline soils could produce good crops of cereals. After the war the subsidies and guaranteed prices encouraged crop growing to continue, but in recent years cereals have declined, rape and other crops have been introduced, and more animals, cattle as well as sheep are to be seen – quietly munching.

Magnificent houses and churches date from the wealthy times of the past, but after the decline of sheep farming starvation and poverty resulted. Little development took place in the villages after the 17th and 18th centuries, which is why so many old buildings survived unaltered. Even the larger houses were sometimes left to stagnate, as was Chastleton House (Walk number 7). The descendants of Walter Jones who built it, were never wealthy enough to add to the original building and so it remained unchanged, though gradually decaying. It has recently been restored by the National Trust, to be seen much as it was in the 17th century.

In recent years wealth has been restored to the region with the social desirability of living in the Cotswolds and the inflow of wealthy potential homeowners from the south east of England, which has pushed up house prices. At the same time there have been huge developments in tourism.

Opinions of the Cotswolds have changed, and the region can no longer be summed up as, 'High wild hills and rough uneven ways', as described in Shakespeare's *Richard II.*

At the beginning of the 19th century, the well known traveller, writer and wit, Sydney Smith, described the area as 'one of the most unfortunate, desolate countries under heaven, divided by stonewalls, and abandoned to screaming kites and larcenous crows'. No one would consider the Cotswolds in those terms today, even though the wintry days can be bleak and raw on the top of the Cotswold plateau.

Area of Outstanding Natural Beauty

Although the boundaries may not be very clear, the location of the characteristic rock is often taken as the extent of the Cotswolds Hills or the Cotswold region A vague boundary can be drawn to coincide with the extent of the rocks, but a more precise boundary has been drawn with the extent of the AONB.

Mainly in Gloucestershire but extending into five other counties, the AONB extends west as far as the border with Worcestershire, south into South Gloucestershire and Wiltshire, north into Warwickshire and east into Oxfordshire, all of which is characterised by the rock type –

limestone. It was traditionally a sheep rearing area, because it was thought that the thin and often stony soils were most suitable for grass and hence for grazing. Field boundaries were created from the local stone and so the landscape of stone walls has evolved. Stone has been quarried in many places and used for building stone - and the stone villages are a well known feature. Not only in the villages has the stone been used, but also in the towns most notably Bath, and much has been transported for use outside the area.

The Cotswolds is the largest of the 41 Areas of Outstanding Natural Beauty in England and Wales. First designated in 1966 with an area of 1555 sq kms, a further 483 kms were added in 1990 - a total of 2,038 sq kms (790 sq miles). Sometimes considered to be Britain's most attractive region, the Cotswolds have certainly achieved a worldwide reputation for scenery. As with all the AONBs, it is protected from major developments. Management is in the hands of the local councils and the Cotswold Conservation Board. Full time rangers are helped in many locations by the Cotswold Voluntary Warden Service, formed in 1968, which helps with such tasks as hedge laying, drystone walling, leading walks or repairing stiles.

The Cotswolds are a walker's paradise, with many miles of paths suitable for short and circular walks, as well as the 102 mile Cotswold Way from Bath to Chipping Campden. Other long distance paths in the region include:

Heart of England Way
100 miles from Cannock Chase to Bourton-on-the-Water

Oxfordshire Way
67 miles from Henley-on-Thames to Bourton-on-the-Water

Wychavon Way
41 miles from Holt Fleet to Winchcombe

Windrush Way
13 miles from Winchcombe to Bourton-on-the-Water

Warden's Way
13 miles from Winchcombe to Bourton-on-the-Water via Upper and Lower Slaughter

Gloucestershire Way
94 miles from Chepstow to Tewkesbury.

Choice of walks

The 20 walks included in this book are chosen to see a wide range of Cotswold towns and villages and to walk across stunning scenery and visit many historic locations. The choice is inevitably subjective, but as the scenery is glorious throughout the entire region, it has often been a particular village, landscape or historic feature which has determined the choice. Such locations as the Roman villa at Chedworth, the old canal at Sapperton, Fairford church, Woodchester Mansion, the amazing water features of the Cotswold Water Park all helped to determine the difficult task of choosing locations to visit.

These walks are not intended to be strenuous. Although a steep hill may be encountered in a few of the walks, for example Wotton-under-Edge, they are mostly gentle walks, and quite short in mileage. The aim is to provide an interesting day out with a short walk, a good lunch in one of the many pubs, and a visit to a feature of interest in the area.

Acknowledgements

My thanks to Margaret as usual for all her work checking the content and clarity of instruction and information. Also many thanks to Gordon not only for accompanying me on these interesting walks but also providing a wide selection of photographs, some of which have been selected to enhance the appearance of the book.

Walk 1
Bredon

This walk is in Worcestershire and begins in Bredon village alongside the River Avon, then circles round the lower slopes of Bredon Hill, past the three attractive villages of Bredon's Norton, Westmancote and Kemerton. Stone buildings, fine gardens and small streams and springs are characteristic of these and other villages surrounding Bredon Hill. An extension to the walk is possible, to reach the summit with its panoramic views.

'To see the coloured counties and hear the larks so high' said AE Housman in 'A Shropshire Lad' – he may have been thinking about Bredon.

Starting point	**Near the church GR 920370, or alongside the River Avon 922373**
Maps	**OS Landranger 150; OS Explorer 190**
How to get there	**Along the B4080 between Tewkesbury and Pershore**
Distance	**6 miles, or 9 miles with the extension to the top of the hill**
Time	**3 hours or 4 hours with the extension**
Terrain	**Level or gently undulating on the main walk**
Refreshments	**Two pubs in Bredon and the Crown Inn at Kemerton (phone 01386 725293)**
Nearest Tourist Information Centre (TIC)	**Tewkesbury (01684 855040)**

Bredon

This old village is one of the ring of villages which surround Bredon Hill, all situated in locations where a water supply was available in the past, and with access to farmland on the hillside as well as farmland of a different kind on the flat plain. Bredon takes its name from *bre* the Old English word for a hill.

Bredon Hill

This hill is a residual, an outlier from the Cotswolds, and is a relic of the time when the Cotswolds extended much further west. The Cotswold scarp is now five miles to the east of Bredon, but was located further west in earlier geological times. Over a period of millions of years, the Cotswolds have been eroded and the location of the scarp has been worn back to its present location. Isolated hills of slightly harder rock have been left behind, like islands on the plain. On the top of the hill is the tower known as Parson's Folly, 39ft (nearly 12m) tall, and constructed in the late 18th century by Mr.Parson of Kemerton Court. He thought the height of 1000ft (305 m) could be reached if he added it to the summit – to give even better all round views. Adjacent to the tower is the Banbury Stone, also known as the elephant stone because of its shape if viewed from one side. The tower and the Banbury stone are both situated inside the hill fort, the outstanding feature of the hilltop.

Bredon Hill from the Malvern Hills on a September evening

The walk

1. From the church of St Giles, pass the Old Rectory as we walk along Dock Lane, passing the large parking area by the River Avon. The river as well as the large open ham on the other bank are popular with a wide range of birds. Keep on to the end of the road, where a track bends right to Mill End Farm and cottage, but our path goes straight ahead, through a gate and along a path between fences, with views to the river. Walk through a small wood to an iron gate, then across the field to a gap in the hedge. Continue across the next field to a stile and a tunnel leading us beneath the railway line. Follow a path through trees to reach a metal gate then cross a small field to reach a road. Keep straight ahead over the road and a stile. Cross the next field, to reach another stile, and a road where we turn left to walk into Bredon's Norton. Pass a few houses and then take the first turn right, by the old chapel. The Norman church of St Giles is on the left, and well worth a visit, and on our right is a footpath signed to Westmancote 1 mile – which is our route for the onward walk.

2. **If wishing to follow the longer extension walk** to the top of the hill, continue along this narrow road and where it bends left, signed Farm Shop, turn right along the track signed Public Bridleway, Bredon Hill 1. On the left is a converted barn and then the magnificent old manor house. The drive bends left after 100 yards, and after a further 50 yards we keep ahead into the field, but veer slightly right to pass alongside the barns. Follow the blue bridleway signs, to walk up to an iron gate at the top of this field. Follow the line of a track, and continue up the hill, passing between two small clumps of trees, to reach another gate. Go on though this and up to another gate and still keep straight on. The track becomes steeper for a short distance, but eases off again before reaching another gate. Beyond this gate the track bends to the right and crosses a wonderful area for wild life: a hummocky area with grasses, undergrowth, and trees. Near the end of the hummocky area turn sharp left just before reaching a wooden gate and climb quite steeply up a broad rocky track. This leads up for 100 yards to a gateway and an open field, where we turn right along the margin of the field. At the end of the field we go through a wooden gate, with a small wood to the right and old quarry workings to the

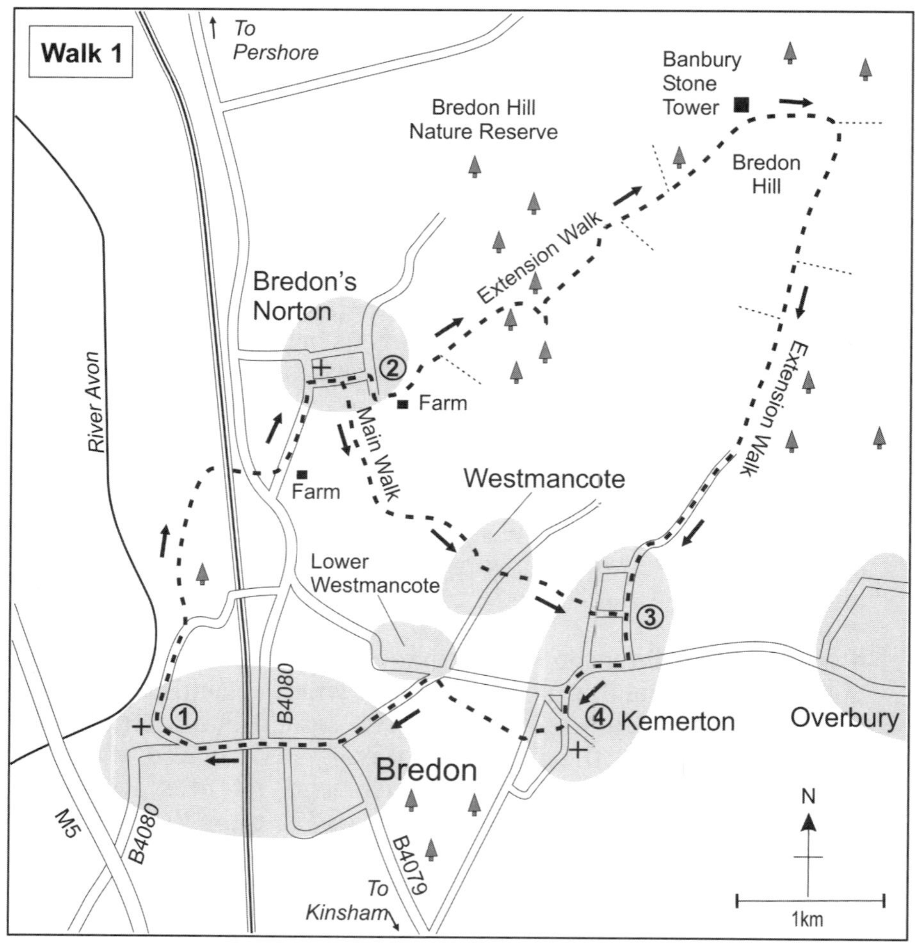

left. At the end of the field, go right, through a small wooden gate into a narrow woodland, The Warren. There is an open field to the right, and a steep wooded slope to the left. Keep going to the end of the wood and emerge to an open field, with a stone wall and steep slope to the left. The tower soon comes into view. Go through a gate and arrive at the embankment and ditches of the old fort. Walk past the tower and then round the edge of the deep hollow in which the Banbury stone sits, looking like an elephant. Walk on towards the wall and turn right, walking past the end of a large ditch and embankment surrounding the old fort. The wall is on the left. Beyond the woodland ahead is the large telecommunications mast. Turn right at the wall just before reaching the woodland and walk alongside the wall on the left. Over to the left, across one field, is Lalu Farm. From here keep more or less straight ahead for about a mile to reach a narrow road, where there are a few parking places. This lane leads towards Kemerton, passing Bell's Castle and several delightful houses.

The main walk continued from point 2

Follow the sign pointing to Westmancote, along the right margin of a field to reach a stile and keep straight ahead with the field boundary now on our left. Pass through two modern metal gates and over a footbridge - into the next field with the hedge on our left. At the end of the field cross over a footbridge and go on through a metal gate and veer slightly left along the left margin of the field. Just before the end of the field go through a gate to the other side of the hedge and along the left side of the field. At the end of this field notice the gate to the Beggarboys Reserve. Turn

Elephant shaped Banbury stone on Bredon hill

right here, just beyond the hedge, and follow the clear path. Climb slightly as we approach the first buildings of Westmancote, and reach a driveway. Manor Farm Barns and Rosecourt Stables are to our right, but we turn left, and walk on to reach the road. Notice the thatched house and other attractive stone houses to our right, and we go straight across here and follow the sign to Kemerton. The footpath stays close to the hedge on our left and the buildings of Kemerton can be seen ahead. At the end of the field go through an old metal gate and a path between gardens, to a narrow road. Keep ahead to a second road and turn right here for about 10 yards and then left along another narrow road, between stone and brick walls and a few houses.

3. At a T-junction we turn right, and join the route followed by the extension walk. Reach a major road, and on the right is a car parking space outside the Catholic church of St Benet. Here is a useful bench, beneath a sorbus tree and close to the stone celebrating Kemerton winning the Best Kept Village competition. Turn right here and walk into the village, passing the village hall, a memorial to Edward VII in 1911. Notice a spring gushing out through the wall on our right, and straight ahead where the road bends is the fine and impressive stone house, The Warren. A few yards further along is the War Memorial. Straight ahead are the shop and pub, The Crown, if required, but we turn left here off the main road. On the wall of the building on the corner can be seen the remnants of the former function of this building, with advertisements declaring that landaus, wagonettes and hunters are available for hire. Follow this road between the houses, passing a small crossroads, and a farm with farmyard, in the village.

Old advert on building

4. When the road bends left, just before the church of St Nicholas, go right through a small wooden gate and walk across the orchard to

reach a wooden gate and the road on the far side. Turn left for 20 yards, then go right through an old iron kissing gate, along a path to the left of scattered trees. On our left in the midst of a large open stretch of parkland are some fine horse chestnuts, as we follow the small marker posts showing the route of the path. Come alongside a wood on our right, as we reach a modern metal kissing gate. Cross a track and keep ahead between fences, with an established wood to our right, and young trees to the left. Continue through a wooden gate and on the well worn path in the wood, to reach a narrow fenced straight path, with young trees on the right and smallholdings through the trees to the left.

Reach the road and turn left to walk into Bredon. Pass the turning left to Cheltenham B4079, then the Village Hall, some new building, two car parks on the right alongside the playing fields, and then the right turn to B4080 Pershore road. Cross over the railway bridge, then pass (or call in) the Royal Oak and Bredon Pottery (on the pottery wall is an old AA sign giving distances to London, Tewkesbury and Pershore). Fork right when the main road bends slightly left. This leads past the post office, several delightful houses and the Fox and Hounds as we return to the church – the spire has been visible for quite a long time. Just beyond the church, towards both the motorway and the river is the Tithe Barn, adjacent to Manor Farm. Along the road near the entrance driveway to the barn is an old, obelisk milepost, dating from 1808, and giving distances to Upton, Pershore, Evesham, Winchcombe, Tewkesbury and Cheltenham.

Obelisk milepost in Bredon

Not to be missed

The church of St Giles Bredon has many Norman features dating from about 1190, and there are interesting heraldic tiles in the chancel, representing many notable families, including the Beauchamps, Fitz Alan, Berkeleys and the Despensers. The tall slender spire is a well known landmark, to be seen from the surrounding countryside as well as by travellers on the M5. It is located near the middle of the cruciform church. Adjacent to the church are several fine buildings, including the rectory, the large 18th century brick stables, the manor houses and the tithe barn, which dates from about 1350.

AE Housman wrote:

In summertime on Bredon
The bells they sound so clear

Presumably a reference to all the churches in the villages surrounding the hill. Fielding in his novel *Tom Jones* made references to Bredon, and in more recent times the local writer John Moore wrote about the imaginary village of Brensham which is based on Bredon.

The Tithe Barn

Now managed by the National Trust the barn is open March to November (phone 01451 844257). It was given to the National Trust by Mr GS Cottrell in 1951, 600 years after it had been built for the Bishops of Worcester. In 1980 a fire swept through the barn, burning the hay and destroying the roof. Several of the 14th century timbers were destroyed, but the building was restored by the National Trust during the next three years. It a formerly associated with the Bredon Manor house, which had to accommodate the bishop and his household whenever they were in residence. The main crops in the 14th century were wheat, barley for malting, peas as winter feed for pigs, wool and hay, all of which were stored in the barn. It was not really a tithe barn but a manorial barn used for storing crops from the manorial farms. The barn is 40.2 metres (132ft) in length and 13.4 metres (44ft) wide, and in one of the porches is an upper room with a fireplace. This was the Reeve's Chamber from where the Reeve could check on deliveries and also keep an eye on the contents as well as the workers.

Walk 2
Chipping Campden

A figure of eight walk from Dover's Hill consists of two short circuits, nearly two miles round Lynches Wood or three miles into Chipping Campden. Either or both of these can be started at the car park on Dover's Hill.

Starting point	**Grid reference 136396**
Maps	**OS Explorer OL 45; OS Landranger 151**
How to get there	**Either B 4035 from Evesham via Badsey, Bretforton and Weston-sub-Edge. Turn left at Weston sub Edge, pass Seagrave Arms and immediately turn right along the narrow road, past the church. This climbs up steeply to Dover's Hill. Or from Chipping Campden at the opposite end of High Street from the church, follow the narrow road which leads up to Dover's Hill**
Distance	**5 miles**
Time	**2-3 hours – though it is easy to spend several hours in Chipping Campden, with restaurants, cafés, the church and the Arts and Crafts Museum**
Terrain	**Gentle in the town, and with only a slight incline up to Dover's Hill as this is the dip slope of the Cotswolds and not the steep escarpment. The circuit round Lynches Wood includes a fairly steep descent and then a climb back up part of the Cotswold scarp to return to the toposcope**
Refreshments	**A very good choice of pubs, cafés and hotels in the town centre**
Nearest (TIC)	**On the High Street opposite the Market Hall (phone 01386 841206)**

One of the most famous and attractive of the Cotswold towns and villages, a small settlement had grown up at Chipping Campden before the Norman Conquest. Chipping is from Old English *cēping*, a market or market-place and Campden probably derived from valley with camps or enclosures. A market charter was granted by King Henry II in 1185 and this contributed to the town's growth. Sheep farming brought prosperity in the 14th and 15th centuries and William Grevel was one of Britain's most successful merchants. A major benefactor in the 17th century was the local lord Sir Baptist Hicks who lived in Campden House - which was burnt down in the Civil War and never rebuilt.

With the decline of agriculture the town declined. But fortunately, with a railway line, and several empty cottages, the town was given a boost by the arrival of members of the Arts and Crafts movement. CR Ashbee considered Chipping Campden ideal for his plans, and he relocated the Guild of Handcrafts here in 1902. He moved from the East End of London with many skilled craftsmen, and set up a workshop in the Silk Mill in Sheep Street. Although most of the craftsmen had moved back to London by 1908, their short stay in the Cotswolds encouraged the growth of the Arts and Crafts movement in this area, making imaginative use of old crafts and producing hand made articles, drawing upon rural areas for ideas and inspiration. The Guild went into liquidation in 1908 but by then the tradition had been established and still continues today. Ashbee left in 1919 and Griggs became the principal figure between the two World Wars.

Colourful Chipping Campden town sign

Dover's Hill was bought by Frederick Landseer Griggs, an etcher and engraver who came to live in Chipping Campden in 1904. He realised the hill was threatened with development for a large hotel. He later passed the hill to the National Trust who have been managing the area since 1929. The hill is named after Robert Dover (1582-1652), a local barrister, who organised the Olimpick Games here in 1612 and they continued, with a few gaps (such as the Civil War) until 1852. They were stopped then for a variety of reasons including rowdy behaviour and some of the games were becoming too violent. They were revived in 1951 and are still held annually – nowadays on the Friday evening after the Spring Bank Holiday. Competitions include sack races, tug of war, and shin kicking.

View to the distant Malvern Hills from Dover's Hill

The walks

1. From the car park and the toposcope walk along the level grassy area, with the steep slope down to the left. After a few yards notice a stile and footpath heading across the field to the right – the route of our walk from Chipping Campden later. Keep ahead towards the triangulation point where the path on the grassy surface divides. The right fork leads to a kissing gate and the footpath heading away from Dover's Hill towards Chipping Campden, but for now take the left fork through a gap in a fence and down a few wooden steps. This leads to a gate and a wall, but turn left just before this field boundary, and head down the grassy slope with a fence and a line of trees on our right. As we descend this area of pasture, look over to the left to see the toposcope and on the slope are hummocks and undulations where

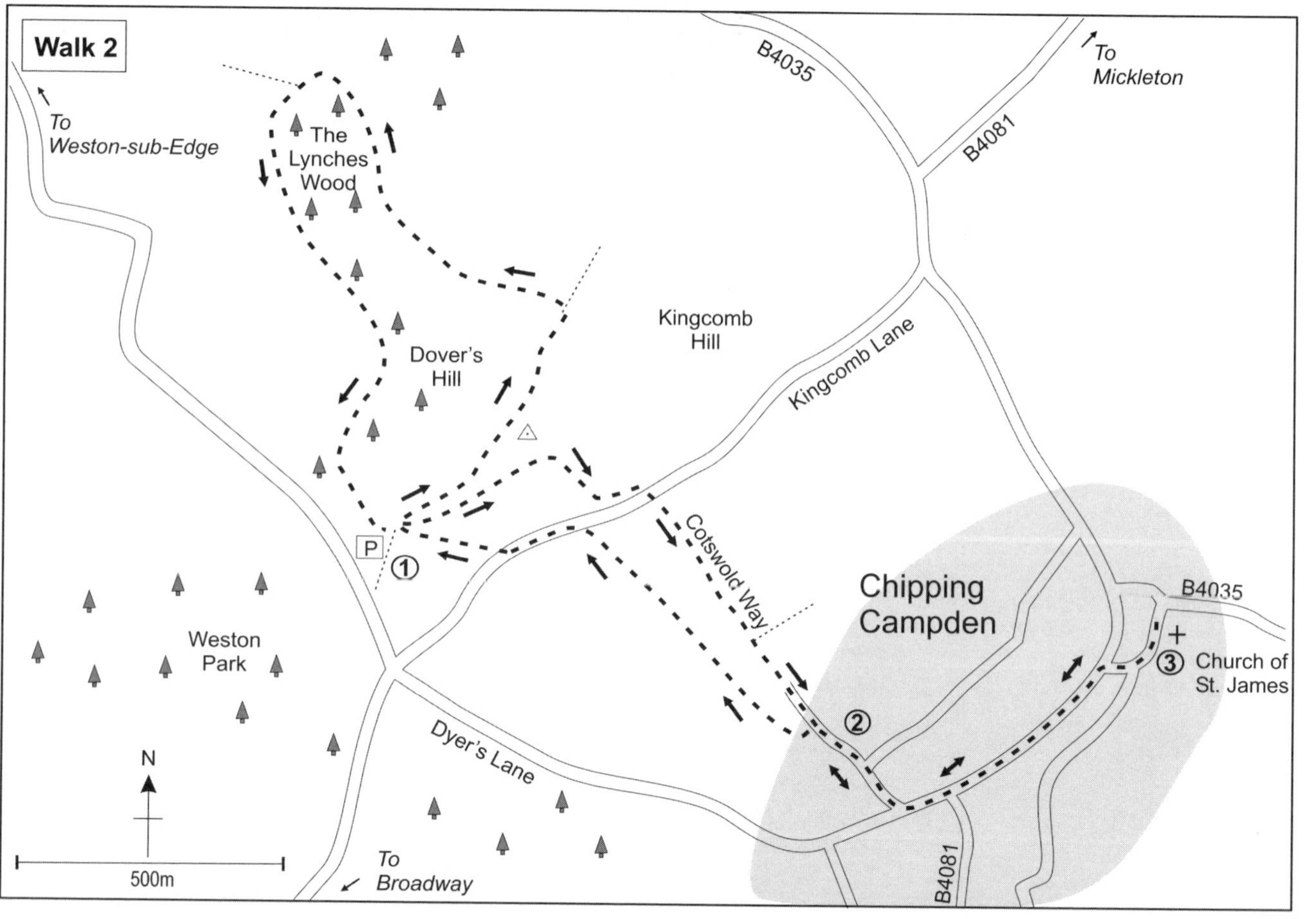

Walk 2
To Weston-sub-Edge
The Lynches Wood
B4035
To Mickleton
B4081
Kingcomb Hill
Dover's Hill
Kingcomb Lane
P
Cotswold Way
Chipping Campden
B4035
Church of St. James
Weston Park
Dyer's Lane
N
500m
To Broadway
B4081

there have been land slips in the past. Stay close to the fence as we descend towards the woods, and enter the woods through a wooden kissing gate alongside a large gate. Lynches Wood is very rich in wild life, noted for oak, ash, sweet chestnut as well as hazel and hawthorn, and wild flowers such as primroses and bluebells are numerous in the spring. Badgers and deer live here and the bird life includes nuthatches, woodpeckers, with summer visiting warblers round the edges.

Follow the very clear path through a few conifers at first and then mixed and mainly deciduous trees. Fairly level at first the path begins to bend round to the left, to reach a National Trust sign by a short stretch of wooden walkway. The path continues to bend left and is joined by a path coming in from the right – now with Cotswold Way Circular Way sign. After descending a little, and still bending round to the left and passing National Trust signs, we reach a few wooden steps and begin to climb. This becomes steeper and we climb up more steps, at the top of which turn right. A short stretch of fairly level walking leads to a kissing gate and the edge of the woods. Out on the grassy area again, the walk is fairly level at first, but then begins to climb quite steadily. Stay close to the woods a few yard to our right as we climb, and then begin to bend to the right, as the woodland margin moves further away. Keep climbing and notice the toposcope on the hilltop ahead and aim in that direction to complete the circuit.

For the onward walk to Chipping Campden

Leave the toposcope, with the steep Cotswold scarp to our left, and a line of trees to our right. Stay close to the line of trees and walk towards the triangulation point. A few yards beyond this on the right is a gate and we turn here, along a narrow path, now following the Cotswold Way. Reach the road and turn left for about 100 yards and then turn right. A clear track leads down to farm barns and then the first rather impressive houses on the edge of Chipping Campden. Pass more of the lovely stone houses and on the right notice three with thatch, the last of which contains a large topiary bird in the garden. We are now at the end of Hoo Lane and its junction with Back Ends. Keep straight ahead to reach St Catharine church.

2. Turn left along the main street, passing many lovely stone houses. A few yards beyond St Catharine School is the Davies House where a plaque tells us that was the birthplace of Ernest Wilson in 1876. He became known as one of the world's largest plant collectors, from all

parts of the world but most notably from China. A Memorial Garden is situated at the far end of High Street, just beyond the turn leading to the church. When the road divides stay on the left side – with the island on our right. Here are restaurants, the Town Hall, War Memorial and the Market Hall. Of many more old buildings on our left, be sure not to miss the Old School House, with the cane logo on the door post, and the weird Punk sculpture on the doorstep. Next is the huge house lived in by Grevel and beyond this we turn right along Church Street. First on the right is Calf Lane with the large old Court House, now a private dwelling. Next we reach a grassy and sunken area, which was formerly a carriage wash pond, where carts could wash their wheels before going along the main street. The Court Barn Museum is also on the right and the old Alms Houses built by Hicks in 1612 are on the left. Just before reaching the church notice the ogee shaped gate lodges, surviving remnants of Campden House. The house, built in 1613 was burnt down by Royalists.

Old School House doorway with cane carving and punk sculpture

Alms houses in Church street

3. Retracing steps from the church, walk back to the High Street. Look ahead at the roof

line and the variety of buildings. This is a very photogenic main street. The town motto is History in Stone – which is most appropriate, as most of the buildings are built from local stone, many dating from 16th 17th and 18th centuries. We pass the Woolstaplers Hall from where there are good views across the road to Grevel's House. Next on our left are the Lygon Arms, Dovers House where Griggs lived from 1906-1930, and the Old Grammar School (now an Antique Shop). The Noel Hotel (one of the oldest inns in the Cotswolds, formerly a 16th century coaching inn) has a carriageway route through the building. On our right by now is the island in the middle of the road, with the Old Market Hall, which was built in 1627 by Sir Baptist Hicks to provide shelter for stallholders selling their local produce. An early example of a farmers' market. It had been owned by the Noel family, descendants of the Hicks, and was bought for the National Trust in 1944 and subsequently re-roofed.

On the next corner is the Robert Welch show room. A few yards along Sheep Street is the old Silk Mill, the location of the starting point of the Arts and Craft Revolution in Chipping Campden when CR Ashbee and his Guild of Craftsmen moved to the town in 1902. A memorial

Market Hall from the inside

plaque near the door of the mill recalls this, and the mill still contains studios used by craftsmen and women, working in gold, silver and glass.

Continue along the main road, back to point number 2.

Turn right at St Catharines Roman Catholic church, and when the road divides, with Back Ends going right (there is car parking here - and it may be used as an alternative starting point for the walk), and Hoo Lane, the route of our walk from Dover's Hill continues straight ahead. But we fork left along Birdcage Walk to begin the gentle uphill walk to Dover's Hill (225m - 738ft). After a few yards of tarmac turn right along a narrow path between hedge and fence. Reach a road and move 20 yards to the left, and then turn right on a footpath. Cross a footbridge over a small stream to reach another road, and keep straight ahead. Go on through a kissing gate into an old orchard - probably with grazing sheep - stay close to the fence and reach another gate then cross the middle of a field - another former orchard. Walk along the edge of a small field to a gate and into a large field, and straight across this to reach a road, Kingcomb Lane. Turn left here and walk along the verge for 250 yards to a footpath sign and here we go right, through an old gate. Cross the field and go over a stile on to the open grassy area at the summit of Dover's Hill. The natural ampitheatre is down below us and the panoramic view opens out across the plain.

Not to be missed

The magnificent 'wool' church of St James mostly dates from the 15th century, but a few earlier fragments have survived. A major donor was William Grevel (who may have been the inspiration for Chaucer's Merchant pilgrim). There is a memorial brass to Grevel, and many other monuments, including the 17th century tomb of the Hicks family in the South Chapel. The approach to the church is along the avenue of lime trees, representing the Apostles. Also in the churchyard can be seen several graves of the Arts and Crafts workers, including Pyment, Gaskin, Sleigh and Russell.

The Arts and Crafts Museum

Court Barn Museum, a museum of Craft and Design. Here can be seen the history of silver, jewellery, bookbinding, printing cabinet making and other crafts.

Opening times are: April to September; Tuesday to Saturday 10.30-5.30 and Sundays 11.30-5.30
October to March; Tuesday to Saturday 11-4 and Sundays 11.30-4
Admission £3.75 or £3 for concessions.

Walk 3
Stanton and Stanway

Views open up across the Worcestershire Plain on the climb out of Stanton, and after completing the climb you can also see across the Cotswold plateau to Broadway tower and Snowshill. The descent is through Lidcombe and Longpark woods into Stanway from where gentle parkland is crossed on the return to Stanton.

Starting point	**Car park close to the Village Hall and cricket pitch in Stanton (grid reference 068343) or, for customers, at the Mount Inn (phone 01386 584318 – grid reference 072342) Also limited parking near the churches in Stanton and Stanway**
Maps	**OS Explorer OL45; Landranger 150**
How to get there	**Along the B4632 south west from Broadway**
Distance	**5.5 miles**
Time	**Up to 3 hours**
Terrain	**Steep climb up the escarpment from Stanton, then level for a short distance before descending to Stanway**
Refreshments	**Mount Inn at Stanton; good choice of pubs, cafés and restaurants in Broadway**
Nearest TICs	**Evesham (phone 01386 446944); Broadway (01386 852937)**

Our walk follows part of the Cotswold Way, which extends 102 miles from Chipping Campden to Bath. This long distance trail stays close to the line of the escarpment, climbing up and down this steep slope several times. Officially opened in May 2007, the route passes many famous locations such as Cleeve Hill the highest point in the Cotswolds (1083ft – 330m), Broadway Tower, the Tyndale Monument, Sudeley Castle, Hailes Abbey as well as the glorious scenery and beautiful stone villages. Long views to the west over the Severn valley can be enjoyed in many places.

Village street in Summer

Stanton

Many of the buildings in this picturesque village are of the attractive yellowish limestone. The church of St Michael and All Angels has three Norman pillars and many other features of interest. On the south wall near the door are ancient stone benches dating from the days when the congregation stood for much of the service. Older worshippers were able to sit on these benches, and this is likely to be the origin of the expression 'the weakest go to the wall'. Beneath the organ loft are medieval pews with poppy heads, and evidence of wear and tear caused by the leads of the sheep dogs brought in by the shepherds and tied up during the services. There are two pulpits in this church, one is late 14th century and the other is from 1684. Sir Philip Stott, who owned the estate and much of the village, from 1906-37, lived in the Jacobean Stanton Court, and restored much of the village and was a major contributor to its present beauty. He also brought in Sir Ninian Comper, a leading church architect, to refurbish the church. Look for his strawberry mark in the east window and transepts.

The walk

1. Walk along the road from the cricket pitch, passing Stanton Court and forking left to the medieval village cross, with a 17th century sundial. Turn left here to visit the church, before continuing along the main street of the village – and beginning to climb slightly. On the right is the Old Manor Farmhouse with a date of 1618 above the door. Pass between glorious stone houses, and before the road rises steeply to the Mount Inn, fork right, signed Cotswold Way. On this corner is the Stott Lantern, reinstated in 2007 thanks to the generosity of Kay Kenyon MBE. Pass between stone houses with some thatch, as we climb slightly. A small stream runs alongside the road, a characteristic sight in many of the Cotswold villages, as the rain falling on the hills sinks underground and emerges in springs near the bottom of the slopes. This good clear water supply is often the reason for the location and growth of the villages. The road becomes a muddy and stony track, as we climb steadily, and emerge into open country. Leave the track, just before reaching a gate, and go right along Cotswold Way, through two small gates, and then the path bends to the right. The path soon divides but we follow the right fork, the clearer route, following the stream and passing a small pool on our right. The path then bends to the left and begins to climb more steeply up the grassy slope. Reach a stile, with staples to help keep a grip, invaluable in muddy conditions which

Stott lantern

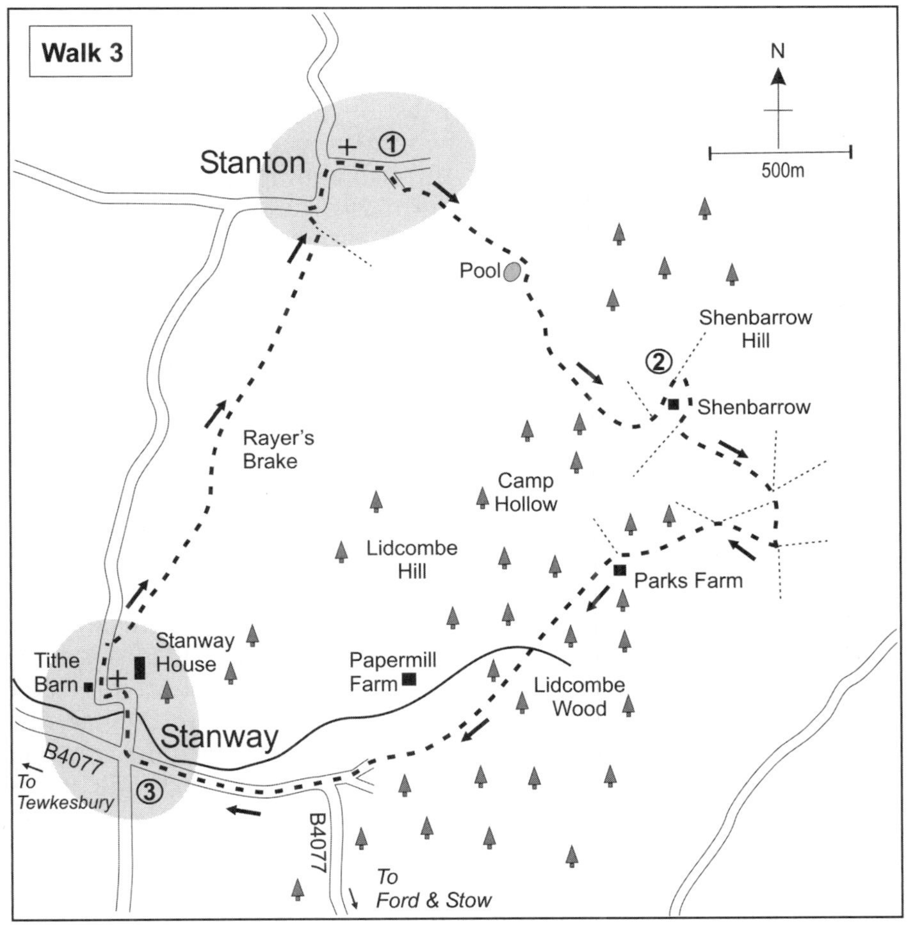

sometimes may be experienced on this walk. Go on over a stile and reach a few trees as we continue to climb through the grass, flowers and gorse. Near the top of the climb, pass through a kissing gate to the left of the Shenbarrow Buildings and cross an open grassy area towards the trees. Notice to our left, the mounds of the Shenbarrow hill fort, dating from about 700 BC.

2. Close to the trees the path divides, with Cotswold Way going straight ahead, but we turn right following the sign for a bridleway – and a blue

arrow. This tracks leads us round to the barns where we turn left, pass through a gate and then right for a few yards, before turning left along a straight path signed bridleway. Walk along the field margin with a wall to our right. Broadway tower will be visible away to the left. At the end of this field go through the gate on to a major track and turn right. Almost immediately pass through another large gate to walk straight along the field margin by the old wall and fence. At the end of the field is a cross tracks, where the left turn would lead to Snowshill, but we turn right here, through a large gate. Walk along the track and after about 200 yards reach another cross tracks. Bend slightly left here, but really keeping ahead on the main track, with woods on our right. Begin to descend, and just before Parks Farm fork right, following a blue arrow. Go downhill, into the woods, crossing the major track, and keeping straight head descending on the muddy and stony track. Bend left at the bottom of the steep slope, but still following the main track. Private woodland is on our left, as we continue along the old track, lined with stones which are uneven in places. Walking through the woodland, rich in wildlife, we descend down the valley, and the noise of a hydraulic ram will be heard pumping away to the left, as we pass over a small stream. On our right is an information display in an old stone building. The information includes mention of the Lidcombe Springs which produce over 200 million gallons of water per annum. The springs were the basis of Stanway's economic prosperity in the Middle Ages when they ran one fulling mill and three corn mills, and later fed the paper mill at the nearby Papermill Farm. Nowadays the water supplies the Stanway House fountain which rises to 300 feet in height, the tallest gravity fountain in the world.

Various paths meet near the information building but we walk straight on along the main track, rising slightly, and with the buildings of Papermill Farm down to the right. The track leads on to emerge from the woods at a few stone houses and the B4077. Walk along the pavement passing a few houses, and a small stream to the right. The Cotswold Way crosses the road here, but we keep straight on to the crossroads to see the War Memorial, with the Bronze of St George and the Dragon by Alexander Fisher and the lettering on the stone carved by Eric Gill. The work of Fisher and Gill can also be seen in the church.

3. Turn right at the crossroads to walk through the village, to Stanway House and the church of St Peter. Walk on along the road, passing a few

houses on the left, with a small stream adjacent to the road. The large tithe barn on the right was built around 1370, by the Abbott of Tewkesbury to store grain and other tithes. It was restored and reroofed by Sir Philip Stott in 1927. Beyond the barn can be seen the Manor House and the pyramid folly on the hillside beyond. On the left of the road here is the cricket pitch, surrounded by a field of ridge and furrow, remnants of which occur in several locations on the rich Liassic clays of the plain. The cricket pavilion is of wood and stands on staddles. It was given by Sir James Barrie who was a visitor to Stanway in the 1920s.

War memorial by Alexander Fisher with stone carving by Eric Gill

Leave the road through an iron gate, opposite the cricket pitch, by following the Cotswold Way sign. After about 30 yards go through another iron gate and along the clear grassy path. The path crosses through parkland where many of the trees are in rows, of horse chestnuts and oak. Cross the first large field to a gate and keep straight ahead across the next field to a gate, climbing slightly. Just keep ahead. The path is on the lower slopes of the scarp, with a scarp up to the right and good views across the plain to the left, with the isolated outlier hills of Dumbleton and Bredon standing up from the plain. Marker posts show the route, and at the end of the next field are two small gates and a footbridge, then another field to another small gate. The church spire at Stanton can be seen straight ahead. After another field and gate, bear slightly left towards a large modern barn, cross some ridge and furrow and reach the gate at the end of the field. Turn left along a surfaced driveway rather than going into a farmyard, and reach the road. Turn right here, and immediately bear slightly left, to walk along the village street, with delightful stone houses, some new thatch and well-kept gardens – a

Stanway House lodge

blaze of colour in spring and summer. At the T-junction, turn left to return to the starting point, or turn right if heading to the Mount Inn.

Not to be missed

Stanway

The church of St Peter, like the houses and tithe barn, is built mainly of ashlars, that is large blocks of stone with smooth faces and square edges. Stanway House is the home of Lord Neidpath, and there has been only one change of family ownership in the last 1270 years. The house is open on Tuesday and Thursday afternoons in June, July and August, when the buildings, interior and extensive gardens can be visited (phone 01386 584469). The landscaped grounds contain an 18th century pyramid folly (a stone belvedere). The Lidcombe springs in the woods behind the house feed a reservoir about 250 feet up the hillside. Over a mile of pipe carries water down to the canal near the house, and feeds the famous fountain, the tallest gravity fountain in the world and also the highest garden fountain in the world. Only commissioned in 2000, the fountain was completed by June 2004, and spouts for 300 feet (91.5 metres).

Close to Stanton and Stanway is Snowshill, one of the National Trust's most popular houses. Charles Wade spent his life collecting a variety of objects, both everyday and rare – and left his total collection to the National Trust. He restored the Cotswold stone house to hold his collection. With views over the surrounding countryside, the terraced gardens and the restaurant all add to the enjoyment of a visit. House and gardens are open from March to October (phone 01386 852410).

Walk 4
Blockley – Batsford

Climbing gently from Batsford Arboretum we cross over the hill and drop down to Blockley in the next valley, then climb up from Blockley for the return to Batsford along a roughly parallel route, through glorious countryside with all round views over the surrounding woods and farmland.

Starting point	In the car park adjacent to the Batsford Garden Centre, Falconry (phone 01386 701043) and Arboretum (phone 01386 701829). Grid reference 183334
Maps	OS Landranger 151; Explorer OL45
How to get there	From the A44 between Broadway and Moreton-in-Marsh, turning off the road just to the east of Bourton-on the-Hill
Distance	6 miles
Time	About 3 hours
Terrain	Gentle climbing across undulating countryside. Clear paths but there may be muddy stretches in the woodland sections
Refreshments	Good choice in Moreton-in-Marsh; pubs in Blockley and Bourton-on-the-Hill
Nearest TIC	Moreton-in-Marsh (phone 01608 650881)

Heart of England Way – is a 101 mile route from Cannock Chase to Bourton-on-the-Water, shown by the logo of a green and white disc with oak trees.

Monarch's Way is a 615 mile long distance path which traces the route followed by King Charles II, and leads from Worcester to Boscobel, then via Stratford and Charmouth to Shoreham. The logo for this route includes the ship *The Surprise*, the Prince of Wales Crown and the Royal Oak at Boscobel.

The Walk

1. Walk back along the drive from the car park, for about 100 yards. When the Lodge House is on the left, turn right here to walk through a wooden gate and across the field to the far right corner. Go over a V-stile at the end of this field, through a few yards of trees, to reach a broad stony track. Good views open up to the left, towards Bourton-on-the-Hill, as we climb slightly. As the track bends round towards the left, we fork right along a narrow path signed Public Footpath and Monarch's Way. Climb steadily, with the stone wall on our right, and we are now on Monarch's Way and Heart of England Way. The path levels off, with an open field to the right, and woods to the left, as we reach a stile and a narrow road. A quick right and then left at the road, but really keeping straight ahead, follow the sign for the two long distance footpaths. Walk along a track through a few trees, and after about 40 yards reach an old iron gate. Beyond this, walk alongside the line of trees on the left margin of a large field. Pass through a gate at the end of the field, or over a stile at the side of the gate, and keep straight ahead. At the end of the next field go through a small gate, turn left, and immediately pass through a large wooden gate. The first splendid views of Blockley can be seen from this point.

Monarch way sign at beginning of walk

2. Walk along a fairly level broad path through a narrow strip of trees. At the end of the first field on our right, turn right over a stile and begin to descend near the right margin of the field, passing a small spring. Our line of walk is towards the church tower down in the valley, and we pass to the left of the smart modernised buildings of Park Farm. Go on down over a stile and bear slightly right, to cross the stony

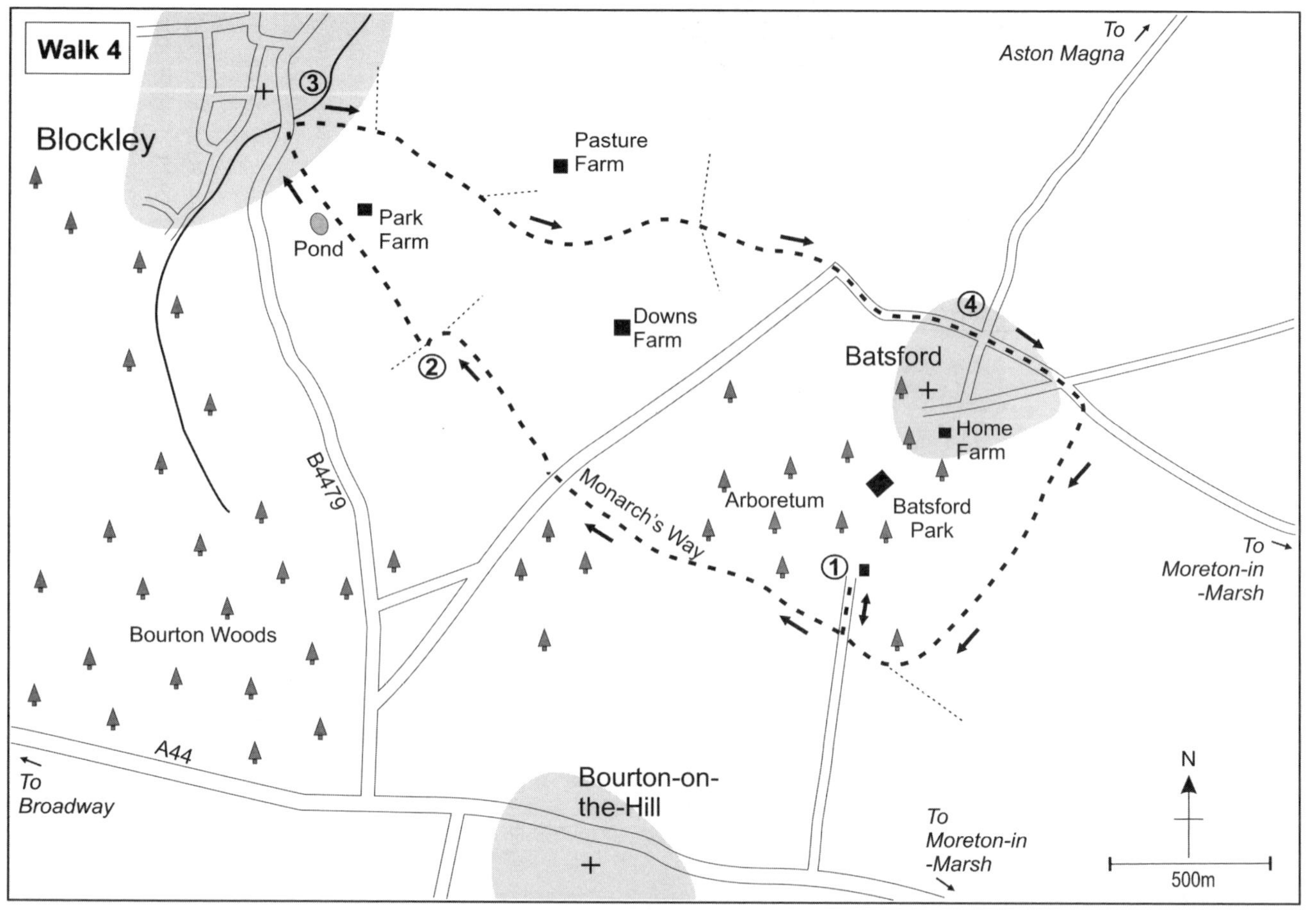
Walk 4
Blockley
To
Aston Magna
Pasture
Farm
Park
Farm
Pond
Downs
Farm
Batsford
Home
Farm
Batsford
Park
Arboretum
Monarch's Way
B4479
Bourton Woods
A44
To
Broadway
Bourton-on-
the-Hill
To
Moreton-in
-Marsh
To
Moreton-in
-Marsh
N
500m
1
2
3
4

View to Blockley down in the valley

drive, still heading towards the church. Pass to the right of an ancient fish pond in a small hollow, which possibly will not contain any water. Go over a stile by the gate at the bottom of the field, and along the right margin of the next field, to another stile and a short track and out to the road – B4479. This is point number 3, and a time of decision. Either turn right for a short cut route bypassing Blockley, and walk along the road as far as the large house named Rose Cottage, then turn right on the narrow lane signposted bridleway and the route to Pasture Farm. Or turn left along the road for the longer route with a circuit round part of the village.

3. Blockley is well worth a visit, so turn left along the road, on the colourful verges, and after about 100 yards, turn right along the narrow road to pass, or visit, Mill Dene Gardens (phone 01386 700457), open only Tuesdays to Fridays, and occasional weekends, from April to September. This is a wonderful garden with interesting plants, created by the owners of the mill, the Dares. The original mill was one

of several in Blockley and was recorded in the *Domesday Book*. In the past it has been used for flour milling, possibly as a wool mill, and also as a piano factory and as a forge. It was subsequently burnt down and rebuilt and the present owners have been here since 1964. Walk on beyond Mill Dene and when the narrow road divides, fork right (no entry for traffic) and climb a short but steep hill, passing the Old School, to reach the T-junction at the top. Here is the main street in the village. A few yards to the left is the Crown Inn, a traditional 15th century Coaching Inn, recently refurbished and offering food and drink to weary or hungry walkers. If ignoring the Crown turn right along the High Street.

Blockley grew in a steep valley, and it is said that the bowling green is the only level patch in this village of golden stone. The Norman church is surrounded by attractive stone houses from the 17th, 18th and 19th centuries as well as former mills. Because of its location in a steep valley, the original wealth of Blockley came from milling, using Blockley Brook which flows into Knee Brook and thence the River Stour. The *Domesday Book* recorded 12 mills, and in later centuries there were six silk mills which were linked with the Coventry ribbon trade and employed up to 500 people. The mills, as well as workers' terraced cottages have now been modernised. Several mill ponds survive and there is an ancient fish pond near Park Farm which we passed on the walk. The church of St Peter and St Paul contains some evidence of the late Norman building, dating from 1180. Just beyond the church is the recent Dovecote and the Bowling Green, but we fork right here past the Village Shop and Café, to walk through the churchyard and descend to the main road. Turn right here, and soon reach Lower Brook House, beyond which is the lane to Pasture farm.

The stony lane towards Pasture Farm rises steadily and has an abundance of wild flowers, noisy bird life in spring and summer, and many butterflies along the verges and in the meadows. The road becomes a stony track and is steep at first, but then levels off. When the track bends left, we fork right to the right side of a large barn and continue uphill alongside the hedge. Notice the buildings of Pasture Farm to the left, and the magnificent views back and left, over Blockley and to Northwick House to the north of Blockley. Go through a small wooden gate and along a narrow, grassy lane which leads into a large field. The route leads on between the hedge on the right, and a wire fence on the left. The path levels off, and we pass through the small wooden gate at the end of the field, over a cross paths – where the left turn is into the Northwick Estate. Keep straight ahead with a hedge on the left. At the end of this field go through a small wooden gate and straight on, but after about 40 yards bear right across the middle of the field to a metal gate, and out on to a narrow road.

Keep straight ahead along this road, and begin to descend fairly steeply.

4. At a small crossroads, Batsford village, the Stud Farm, and church stand to our right. Our onward route is straight ahead, and after about 300 yards, just beyond the next crossroads, look for the gate and footpath on the right. Turn here to walk along a broad path between lines of trees. Emerge into an open field on our left, with views across the fields towards Moreton-in-Marsh. To the right are fields, probably with horses, and the buildings of Batsford village. Keeping straight ahead pass a stile and then a gate with stile alongside. On our right now is the large wire fence surrounding the deer park – and probably sightings of some of the red deer. Across the park is the magnificent

Red deer in the arboretum park

Batsford House, built 1889-92 following the inheritance of the estate by Bertram Mitford in 1886 (and after demolishing the earlier Georgian house).

The parklands include the arboretum, developed in the 1860s by Algernon Freeman Mitford, who later became the first Lord Redesdale. It was his second son David who took over and he was the father of the famous Mitford sisters. In 1919 the house was sold to pay Death Duties, and was bought by Gilbert Alan Hamilton Wills, who later became the 1st Lord Dulverton. The house was donated to a charitable Trust in 1984 but previously Lord Dulverton and his wife had made many additions to the Arboretum.

At the next large wooden gate go into an open field and to a cross paths. Turn right here and walk along the field margin to the Lodge House we saw earlier. At the driveway turn right to return to the car park and our starting point.

Not to be missed

Sezincote House

Gardens open January to November - Thursdays, Fridays and Bank Holiday Mondays from 2.30-5.30, and the house is open from May to September on the same days and times. Sir Charles Cockerell began to redesign an existing house at Sezincote about 1805, using some of his fortune made with the East India Company. He was helped by his brother, Samuel Pepys Cockerell, an architect, who had already designed a house at Daylesford for Warren Hastings. The artist Thomas Daniel, who had lived in India, helped with the Oriental influences in the design of this unique Indian house, and Humphry Repton was involved in both the house and the park. Similarities with Brighton Pavilion can be seen and the Prince Regent is known to have visited Sezincote. Another famous visitor was John Betjeman who gave a glowing account of Sezincote in his poem *Summoned by Bells.*

Batsford

Batsford village is accessible along a minor road from Moreton-in-Marsh, though the Arboretum, Garden Centre and Falconry are all reached from the main A44. A huge development project has recently taken place at the Garden Centre. The small village of Batsford is really part of the estate and contains a few houses adjacent to the church. The church of St Mary was rebuilt in the 1860s, and has a tall spire and an attractive apsidal east end to the chancel. The interior contains many memorials to the Freeman-Mitford-Redesdale family, and in the porch is the memorial to the 2nd Baron Dulverton.

The Arboretum dates back to the Freeman family in the early 17th century, but later much was added by the 1st Lord Redesdale who travelled widely - and collected. It was designed and laid out by Bertie Mitford, the first Lord Redesdale in the 1880s. He was influenced by his time at the British Embassy in Tokyo, which is the reason for the Japanese features to be seen. Many changes were made in the 20th century, but also in the last 30 years by the present owner, Lord Dulverton. He has added many trees notably magnolias and maples. An outstanding monument is the large bronze Buddha at the top of the hill.

Walk 5
Winchcombe

From the historic town of Winchcombe the walk takes us up a steady climb to the Neolithic barrow of Belas Knap on top of the Cotswolds, before walking down to the valley for the return to Winchcombe.

Starting point	**In the car park in the centre of the town close to the Public Library. Grid reference 024283. Parking fee £1 for the day**
Maps	**OS Landranger 163; Explorer OL45**
How to get there	**Along the B4632 Cheltenham to Stratford road and follow signs to the long stay car park**
Distance	**8 miles**
Time	**Up to 4 hours. Short cut version is possible**
Terrain	**Clear paths though patches may become muddy in wet weather; climbing in the first half of the walk with descent and level walking in the second half**
Refreshments	**Very good choice in Winchcombe, with hotels and pubs on High Street and North Street, and tea shops on Hailes Street**
Nearest TIC	**Winchcombe: Phone 01242 602925**

Winchcombe was capital of its own county until it became part of Gloucestershire in the 11th century. Belas Knap is evidence of early settlement in this area, and there are several sites of Roman villas nearby. King Offa founded a nunnery here in 787 AD and later this was refounded as a Monastery. The town was mentioned in the *Domesday Book* and really flourished in the 13th and 14th centuries with the wool trade. St Peter's church was built around 1465, and is one of the Cotswold's finest, with

Busy main street of Winchcombe at end of Cowl Lane

an imposing perpendicular spire and 40 comic gargoyles on the exterior. Winchcombe was the home of Mercian royalty, and in Saxon and Medieval times was one of the richest towns in the region. Nowadays, this thriving small town is a major tourist attraction, set in glorious scenery, with a station on the Gloucestershire-Warwickshire railway from Toddington to Cheltenham racecourse, a nearby pottery, Sudeley Castle and the Folk and Police Museum as well as the noted Railway Museum.

Sudeley Castle is open to the public (daily from 10.30-5) from the end of March until the end of October and contains many relics of history, as well as being surrounded by several distinctive gardens including the Queens' Garden with its old fashioned roses, and a Herbal Garden introduced in 2010. The original owner was Ethelred the Unready, but much of the present castle was rebuilt by Ralph Botelier in the time of Henry VIII. It was later added to by Sir Thomas Seymour, Baron Sudeley, who married Katherine Parr after Henry VIII died. Destroyed by Cromwell, the castle became derelict for 200 years until bought by the Dent family in 1837. The Dent brothers, famed for glove making in Worcester, restored much of the house, and this work was continued by Emma Brocklehurst, the wife of their nephew, John Coucher Dent. Still in the hands of the same family the castle is the family home of Lord and Lady Ashcombe. (Phone 01242 602308)

Belas Knap is a long barrow dating back to about 2500 BC - used for burials possibly for several centuries. At one end is a false entrance, possibly to discourage or confuse grave robbers. The mound has an approximate north-south orientation, and is 178 feet long, up to 60 feet wide and up to 18 feet high. The mound is built of limestone blocks and contains four burial chambers, in which have been found human remains as well as animal bones, flint implements and pottery. The lintels and much of the dry walling were rebuilt on the original lines in 1863-65, when the barrow was first explored. Between 1928 and 1931 the walling was secured, three of the chambers were covered and the contour of the mound was restored. The name of Belas Knap is derived from Saxon words for a beacon or a hill.

The walk

1.

Walk from the corner of the car park along Cowl Lane - passing the old Village Hall. Where the lane joins the High Street you can see the first of many plaques likely to be seen, while in Winchcombe, giving a little history. At the High Street we turn right for the walk, but first, a stroll to the left will take us past Wesley House, where John Wesley is thought to have stayed, in March 1779, and along to the Tourist Information Centre and the Police Museum (open Monday to Saturday 10-5, but closed for lunch).

The right turn takes us along the main street, lined with some fine stone buildings. On the left note the Dent almshouses, built in 1865 by Mrs Emma Dent - and designed by Sir George Gilbert Scott. Further along the road on the right, are the church and at number 23 Gloucester Street is the Railway Museum. But our walk takes us down to the left along Vineyard Street. This tree lined road leads to Sudeley Castle and the site of the former vineyard. A wall plaque tells us that this road was also known as Duck Street because evidence of a former ducking stool has been found. Delightful stone houses line this street. Pass over the stream, the River Isbourne, along which there were formerly several mills, and a few yards further on the right is an old iron kissing gate,

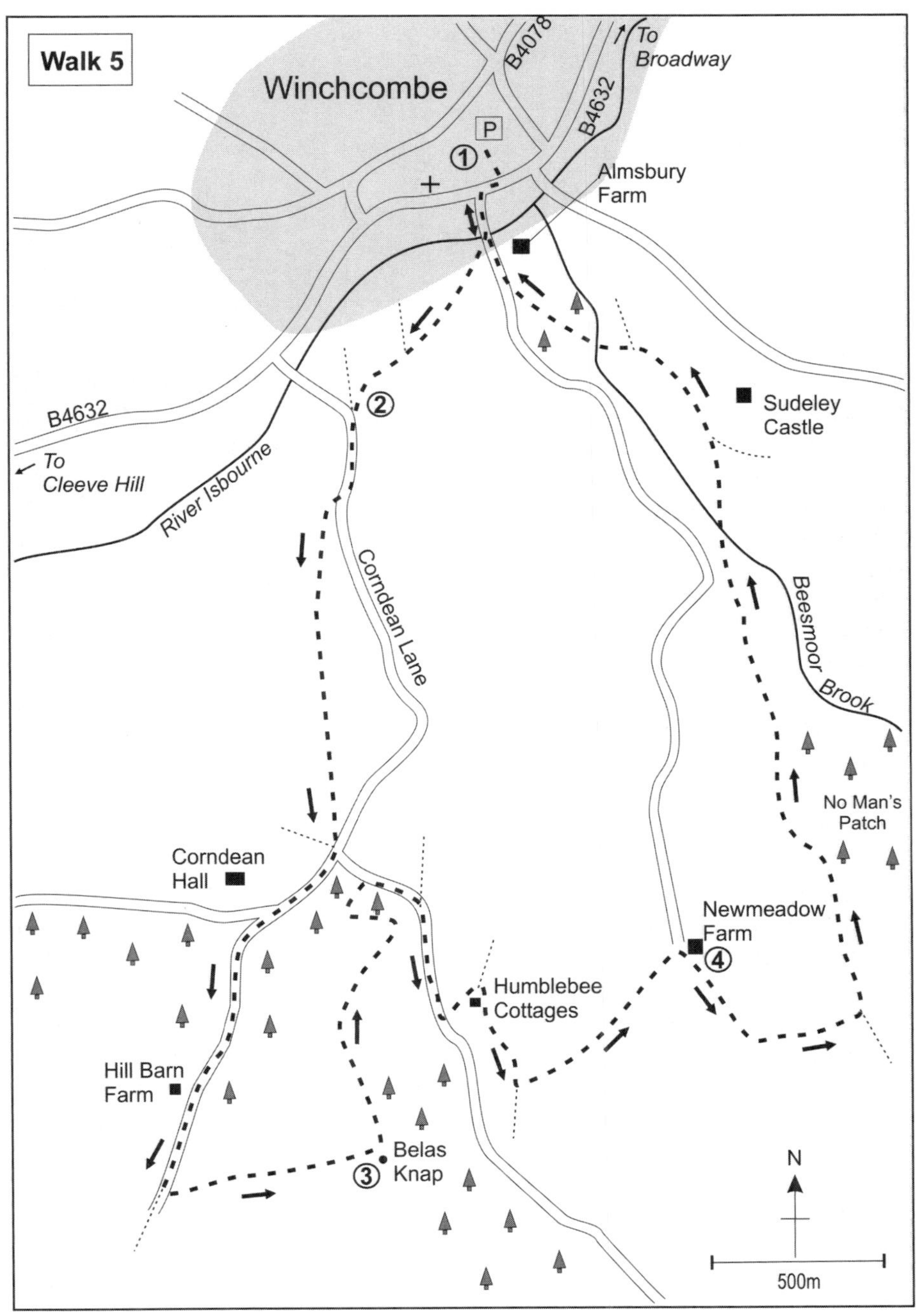
Walk 5
Winchcombe
B4078
To Broadway
B4632
P
①
Almsbury Farm
B4632
To Cleeve Hill
②
River Isbourne
Sudeley Castle
Corndean Lane
Beesmoor Brook
No Man's Patch
Corndean Hall
Newmeadow Farm
④
Humblebee Cottages
Hill Barn Farm
Belas Knap
③
N
500m

View to Winchcombe Church

with a sign for the Cotswold Way. Turn here, and head straight ahead across the field, with very good views right to the church.

2. Reach a narrow road, Corndean Lane, and turn left. After about 300 yards at the entrance to Corndean Hall, go right - signed Cotswold Way and Public footpath to Belas Knap. Follow the driveway, passing the cricket pitch, and then a horse training area on the right. Then on the left is the sign to Cotswold Way, and we go through the kissing gate and walk up the large field - possibly accompanied by fine, sleek, thoroughbred horses. At the top of the field reach a gate in the stone wall, and a road junction. Fork right here, not along the road towards Belas Knap. Climbing slightly the road divides and we fork left, still climbing. Pass to the left of the buildings of Hill Barn Farm and emerge on the top of the Cotswolds, with good views across the right to Cleeve Common and the highest point in the Cotswolds at 330m (1083ft). From Hill Barn Farm continue along a stony track and after about 300 yards the path divides and we turn left to Belas Knap, along the Cotswold Way.

On our left is a tumbledown stone wall, backed in part by a fence which will be much cheaper and easier to maintain, though not as attractive as the stone wall. At the end of this large field is the mound of Belas Knap, and all around here are likely to be the noise of singing birds in spring and early summer – skylarks, pipits, warblers – with a buzzard floating overhead. At the end of the field go over a stone stile to Belas Knap.

Belas Knap: close up of old entrance

3. Leave Belas Knap over a stone stile and immediately turn left to pass through an iron kissing gate. Follow the path alongside the stone wall to the right. The wood, sloping down beyond the wall has a carpet of dog's mercury and bluebells in spring. When the wood ends, still keep going alongside the stone wall, as good views open up to the right to Winchcombe and Sudeley, and then to Hill Barn Farm and Cleeve Hill on the left. Pass through an old black kissing gate, and drop downhill alongside the wall. At the bottom turn left, still following the field margin, now a fence with a wood beyond. At an iron kissing gate, turn right along a sunken track into the woods and descend to the road, where there is a small car parking area. Go over the stile, which has staples to improve the grip of muddy boots, onto the road.

   Turn right here, along the narrow road, pass a footpath going left, and in the open field on the left is a small walled area with trees, the site of a Roman Villa. Turn left at the end of this field, along a stony driveway signposted Cotswold Way. Walk down to the houses, Humblebee Cottages, and the Cotswold Way goes straight on down the slope. For a short cut route keep straight ahead here, following the Cotswold Way 2 miles back to Winchcombe.

   But for the main walk (a further 3.5 miles) we turn right just beyond the buildings, to walk along the front of the stone cottages, and the interesting old outhouse buildings. Continue along the edge of the field, with a wood to the right. Near the end of the wood, at a gate, the official footpath ends, but a track which was formerly an old road goes straight ahead and another turns left. We turn left here to walk alongside the fence, going downhill, then through a gate and another field to the bottom of the slope, and the delightful cluster of houses and Newmeadow Farm. Notice the old sign advising drivers that the old road we have come along is unsuitable for traffic.

4. Turn right here, along a stony track. Pass an iron gate and keep ahead between a hedge and a fence, then descend a slope and cross over a stream which is piped. Climb slightly and come out on to a large, open field. Keep on the track as it bends left and comes round to a T-junction. Here the track bends right, but we turn left along the path, following the yellow arrow with a circle half of green and half of white.

   The path leads across the flat field, with a small valley and a line of assorted trees to our right. At the end of the field, go down slightly to a valley lined with small trees, cross over a small stream, and a stile. Keep straight head. The next field is small and we go over the stile or through the iron gate alongside and into a larger field. The wood named No Man's Patch is on the right. Keep straight ahead over stiles and through fields with the wood just to the right.

   Once past the end of the wood, keep straight ahead, but now across the middle of the field. Pass through the gate at the end of this field, and go slightly right to the far corner of the next field, moving nearer the stream. Leave this field over a stile by a gate and turn right to follow the Windrush Way across the stream, Beesmoor Brook, a tributary of the Isbourne. Then turn left through a kissing gate, cross a small piped stream and head into Sudeley Park, going towards a marker post, with the towers of the castle visible straight ahead. Pass to the left of the house and go through a kissing gate. The path splits here and we fork left, with the children's playground area to our right. Follow the fence to a gateway and then we reach the main drive. Turn left here and walk towards Winchcombe, passing between two pools and fields yellow with daffodils and celandines in the spring. Reach the Lodge House, pass Almsbury Farm and walk along Vineyard Street and up on to Winchcombe High Street.

Not to be missed

Railway Museum

Situated at No. 23 Gloucester Street this museum stretches through an attractive and very productive garden and contains Timothy Petchey's amazing collection of railway memorabilia including relics of lines and companies no longer in existence. This ongoing and increasing collection is operated by a trust and any profits are ploughed back into the collection. Much of the work is done by volunteer helpers and enthusiasts. It is a wonderland for railway enthusiasts. Phone 01242 609305

St Peter's church

On the exterior are bullet holes on the belfry tower, a relic of the English Civil War. Inside the church is a 12th century chest, made by hollowing out an oak log, and an altar cloth decorated by Katharine of Aragon. The two huge stone coffins came from the Abbey church of St Mary the Virgin and St Kenelm, and are thought to contain the bodies of King Kenulf and his son King Kenelm, Mercian kings of the 9th century. Note the collection of old tiles, lifted from the floor for safe keeping, and possibly dating from the 14th century, that is earlier than the building of the church in the 1450s. Near to the tiles is the 1547 alms box with three locks, to prevent vandalism and thieving – not only a modern problem!

Walk 6
Guiting Power

We cross glorious undulating countryside in an area more important for cereal production at present than the more traditional sheep farming, and also pass through two of the loveliest of the many stone villages in the Cotswolds.

Starting point	**At the small car park on Critchford Lane near Kineton and Guiting Power. Grid reference 0842158. Alternative parking is available near the Village Hall in Guiting Power**
Maps	**OS Explorer OL45; Landranger 163**
How to get there	**From the B4077 between Tewkesbury and Stow-on-the-Wold, turn right in Ford, along the minor road, bypassing Temple Guiting to reach Kineton. Turn right at the crossroads along Critchford Lane. After nearly a mile, cross through the ford and climb slightly to reach the car park close to a barn on the left**
Distance	**6 miles**
Time	**Up to 3 hours of comfortable walking**
Terrain	**Undulating walk, mostly on dry and firm paths, though may be muddy near the streams**
Refreshments	**Pubs in Kineton and Guiting Power**
Nearest TICs	**Stow-on-the-Wold (01451 870150) and Winchcombe (01242 602925)**

The name Guiting is probably derived from Old English meaning a flood or a torrent. In the past the upper part of the River Windrush was known as the Guiting. Power is taken from the name of a local family. Guiting Power is the name of a hymn tune by John Barnard, who was inspired to write this piece (for Michael Saward's hymn *Christ Triumphant*) whilst on honeymoon in the Cotswolds. The village retains a few shops, as well as two pubs, the Farmers Arms (0451 850358) and Hollow Bottom (01451 850392). The church of St Michael has a Norman nave and the chancel was added in the 12th and 13th centuries. Increasing population in the village and resulting larger congregations led to the building of north and south transepts which changed the church into cruciform shape. The tower was built in the 15th century and at the same time the walls of the nave were raised, and are supported, by six carved stone corbels. The whole church was restored in 1903. Some of the ancient features were retained, including the two Norman doorways - one now blocked off. A rather sad child-sized sarcophagus can be seen close to the font. The main entrance to the church is the south door, with its wonderful carved arch and decorated tympanum.

The walk

1. Walk back to the narrow road and turn left, going downhill along the broad stony track - Wardens Way. After a short downhill section climb slightly through a few trees to emerge into the open fields with good all round views. A level stretch leads on towards a few buildings and when we reach a driveway turn left, alongside the hedge, signed Wardens Way. The large barn stands a few yards to the right. A narrow stony path leads into the wooded area and descends quite steeply towards the stream, a tributary of the Windrush. Just before reaching the stream, bend right and follow the path through the trees. The stream is on our left, as we begin to climb steadily and emerge from the trees into a more open area. Pass a post with an arrow and W (for Wardens Way) and reach the first house of Guiting Power and a narrow road, with wild flowers along the verges. Walk on between houses with productive and colourful gardens, to reach a T-junction. To the right can be seen the small chapel but we turn left into the village centre. The Green with its World War I War Memorial, is surrounded by stone houses and on the left is the Old Post Office, now a small shop offering coffee and cakes, but primarily an interior design and furnishings shop. The old village pump can be seen on the edge of the Green. Our onward route is along the narrow road - a cul-de-sac, a few yards beyond the Post office, but first follow the sign for Wardens' Way to pass the school and Village Hall if wishing to visit the church. St Michael's church was formerly nearer the centre of the village, but

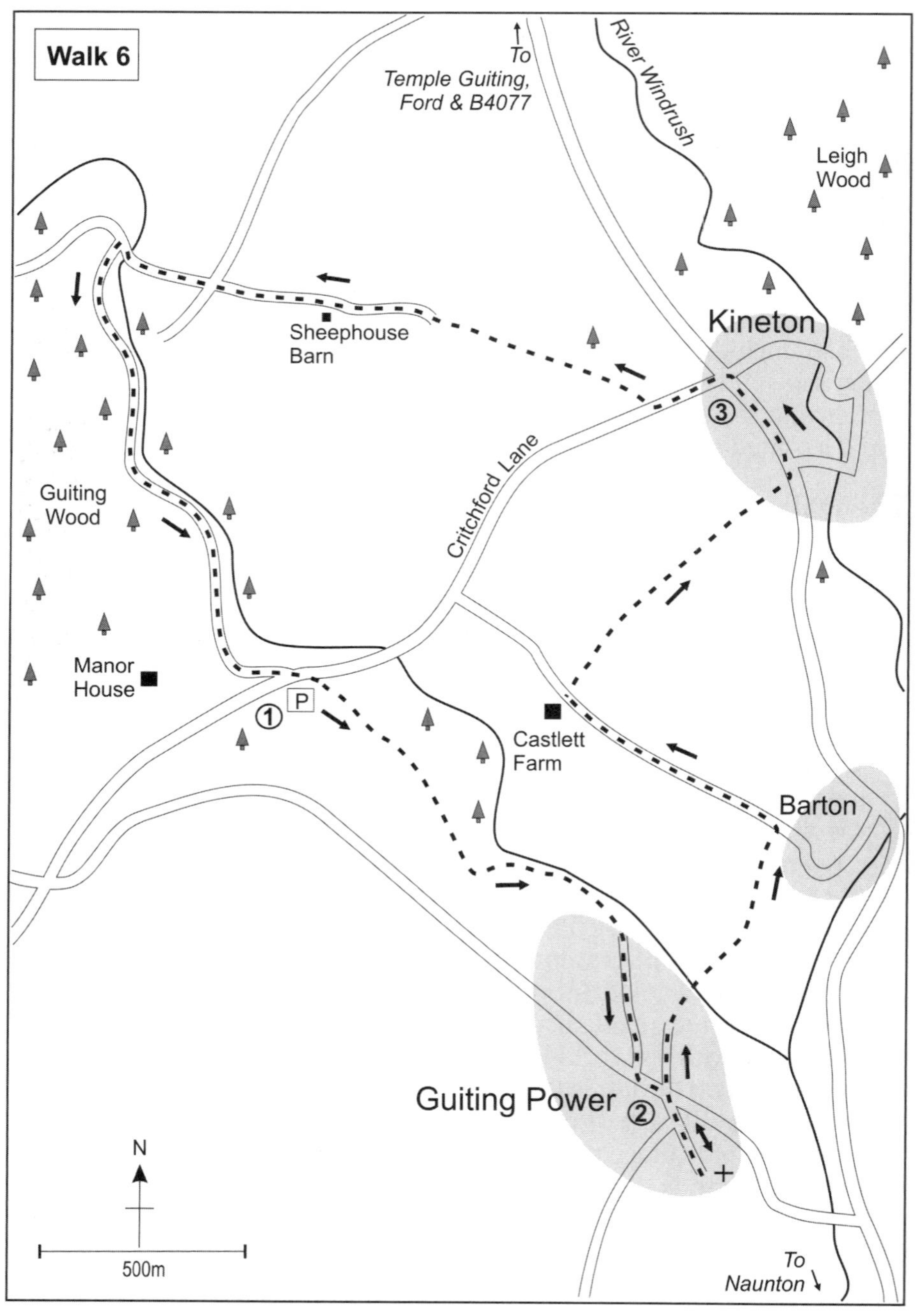
Walk 6
To
Temple Guiting,
Ford & B4077
River Windrush
Leigh
Wood
Sheephouse
Barn
Kineton
3
Critchford Lane
Guiting
Wood
Manor
House
1
P
Castlett
Farm
Barton
Guiting Power
2
N
500m
To
Naunton

Old Post Office

several cottages have disappeared to leave the church on the edge of the village.

2. Retrace steps and just before reaching the Old Post Office turn right along the narrow road, passing between more of the local stone houses. At the end of this road go on through a wooden kissing gate signed Public Footpath and pointing straight ahead. Pass alongside the small pool on the right of the path and walk close to the stream, with a wood on the right. At the end of the field cross a footbridge over the small fast flowing stream in a lush wetland area, then climb to the top of the slope. The path divides but we fork left through a wooden kissing gate and go straight ahead along the margin of the field, with a hedge on our right. Reach a wooden kissing gate and emerge onto the narrow road. The small hamlet of Barton is a few hundred yards to our right, but we turn left along the road. After nearly a half mile, with the magnificent Castlett Farm buildings on our left, and a house

on our right, we turn right at the gate just beyond this house on the right. Walk to the left of the house through a part of the garden and keep straight ahead over a stile and along the margin of the field, between a hedge and a fence. Climbing very gently we reach a one rung stile with a carefully placed stone placed to aid walkers with short legs. Keep straight ahead, on the left side of the hedge, along the margin of a level and large field. At the end of this field continue ahead and descend to the road and Kineton.

3. Turn left to walk through the village, with neat houses and colourful gardens – and nothing more colourful than the hanging baskets at the Halfway House, a Donnington pub (phone 01451 850344). At the end of the village, turn left at the crossroads towards Roel and Charlton Abbotts. After about 200 yards along this road, at the end of the first field, turn right along a clear track – signed unsuitable for vehicles. With a slight steady climb at first, but then levelling off, remarkable all round views can be enjoyed for several miles in all directions, across the undulating landscape towards Winchcombe and Snowshill. After nearly a mile we reach a narrow road. Just keep straight ahead along this road to descend quite steeply to the river valley. Shortly after a sharp right bend the road divides. The straight ahead option begins to climb, but we turn left to walk alongside the river. The stream and lush wetland vegetation and trees are on our left, and to the right is Guiting Wood. Wild flowers are numerous on both sides of the road. The narrow road winds and undulates for a mile and we reach the lone house – Pump Bottom Cottage. Wardens Way joins us from the right and also on the right can be seen the impressive Manor House. We then climb up to a road junction and the parking place for our starting point, close to a barn (with nesting swallows) and small sheep enclosure.

Not to be missed

The church at Temple Guiting has ancient links with the Knights Templar who owned this manor in the 12th century. The church, which dates from that time, is a short distance out of the village. The Medieval glass in the middle window on the south side of the nave dates from 15th century or early 16th and contains figures of St Mary Magdalene, St James the Lesser and St Mary the Virgin. There were originally 12 panes in this window but part was sold for £5 and is now located in the Metropolitan Museum of Art in New York. Also on the south side is the 18th century hatchment, part of the Heraldic Memorial of the Reverend George Talbot who was responsible for the alterations to the church in the mid 17th century. Other features of interest are the Georgian Decalogue, dating from circa 1748, located over the south door, and the Arms of George II, made in plaster by John Switzer in 1742, and now located above the entry to the Bell Tower. A medieval winged lion corbel is located in the chancel and a rather grotesque headed corbel is seen in the porch. Changes to the church have been ongoing and a major period for change was in the 19th century. Most recently has been the addition of the Tom Denny window, a Memorial to Lord Butterworth and based on *Psalm 111* 'the fear of the Lord is the beginning of wisdom'.

Cotswold Farm Park one mile east of Kineton and one mile south of the B4077, is a very active farm with crops and animals but also is the home to a collection of rare breed animals including Cotswold sheep and Gloucester cattle. There is a playground area for children, and also a touch barn, as well as a wild life walk, cafe and shop. Open daily from March to September, 10-30-5 (phone 01451 850307) and also open weekends and the half term week in October.

Walk 7
Adlestrop – Daylesford – Oddington

From the stone village of Adlestrop cross glorious countryside as we walk past Daylesford Hill Farm to Lower Oddington, with its remarkable doom painting, before reaching Adlestrop Park as we return towards Adlestrop church.

Starting point	**At the Village Hall (box for payment). Grid reference 242272**
Maps	**OS Explorer OL45; Landranger 163**
How to get there	**Along the A436 from Stow-on-the-Wold towards Chipping Norton and after three miles turn left signed to Adlestrop**
Distance	**6 miles**
Time	**3 hours**
Terrain	**Gently undulating across fields and along lanes**
Refreshments	**Very good food on offer at the pub in Lower Oddington and a wide choice of cafés, restaurants and pubs in Stow-on-the-Wold**
Nearest (TIC)	**Stow-on-the-Wold (01451 830352)**

Adlestrop

The delightful stone village of Adlestrop still retains a small shop and Post Office close to the church. The church clock and the entrance gates commemorate Queen Victoria's Golden and Diamond Jubilees. The clock is unusual in having only two faces, on the two sides visible from the village. Of the main structure, only the chancel arch (13th century) and the tower (14th or 15th century) are earlier than the 18th century. The font dates from the 15th century. A church has existed on this site for many centuries but it was rebuilt in the 18th century and major changes took place in the 19th century. In the church and churchyard are monuments to the Leigh family, who have owned Adlestrop Park since the 16th century. Adlestrop Park was laid out by Humphry Repton.

Adlestrop House is a 17th century building and was visited by the novelist Jane Austen (1775-1817) at least three times between 1794 and 1806. The Reverend Thomas Leigh (1726-1813) was her mother's cousin. Some of the Adlestrop scenery and events noticed during her visit in 1806 are the basis of several parts of *Mansfield Park.*

The walk

The old railway sign in the bus shelter

1. From the Village Hall turn left and walk along the road. The road divides by the shelter with the old Great Western Railway sign for Adlestrop – the station made famous by Edward Thomas. It was the chance occurrence of a poet being in a train which made an unscheduled stop at Adlestrop station. One of the most famous of the War Poets, who was killed in 1917, this was not one of Thomas's major works, but it has become a memorable poem in the life of Adlestrop village.

   Yes. I remember Adlestrop
   The name, because one afternoon
   Of heat the express train drew up there
   Unwontedly. It was late June.

   Take the left fork here and walk along the road, rising slightly. After 200 yards, look for a stile on the right, and leave the road here to follow the winding path through a narrow strip of deciduous woodland, walking roughly parallel to the road on our left. Keep going as far as a wooden gate and the main road where we turn left for a few yards. Pass the road signed to Adlestrop and opposite this is West Lodge. A few yards beyond the lodge and before the road to Cornwell is a footpath. Turn here to walk through a small area of woodland and reach a fenced field where we turn right. This leads us to the main

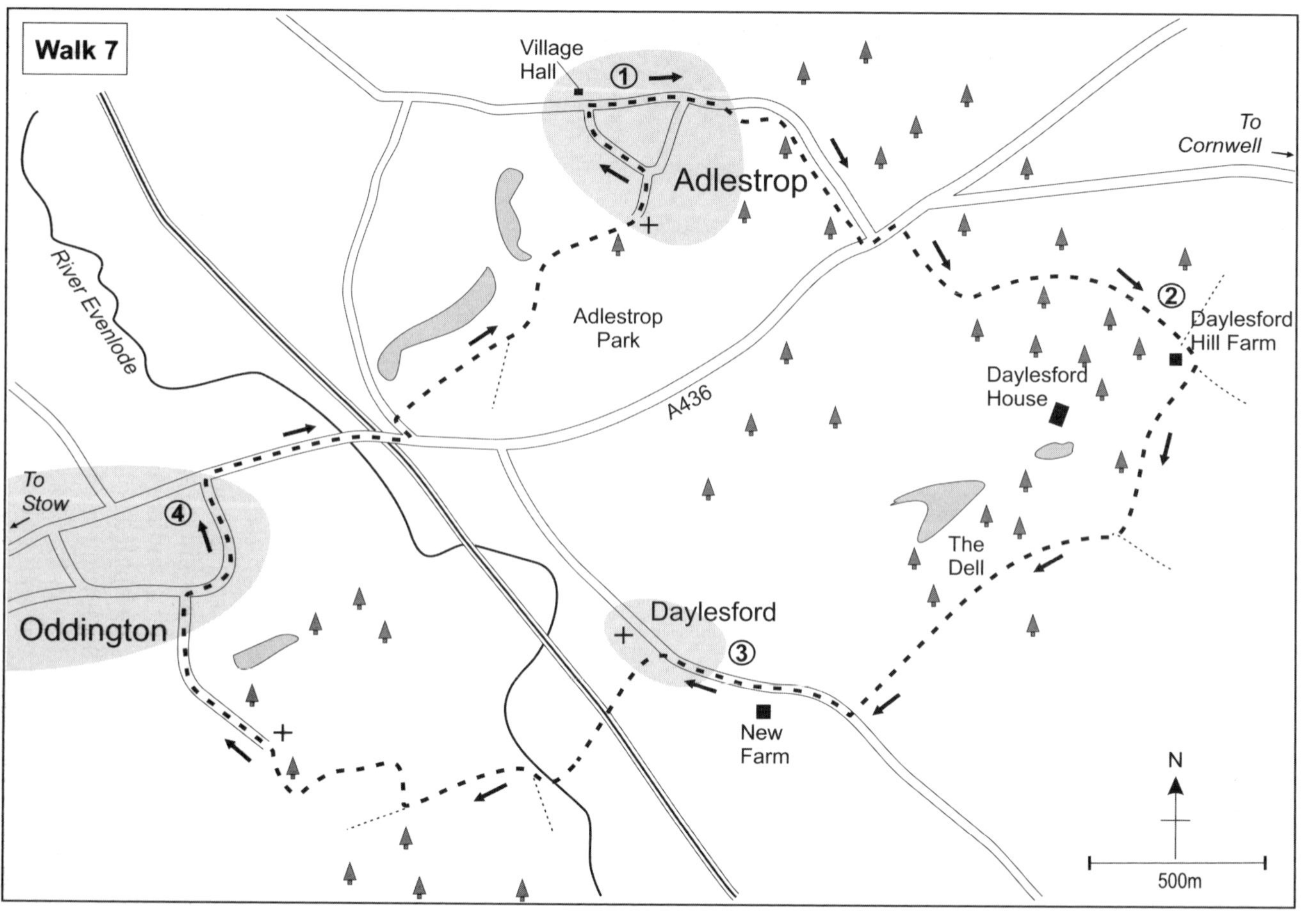
Walk 7
Village Hall
①
Adlestrop
To Cornwell
River Evenlode
Adlestrop Park
②
Daylesford Hill Farm
Daylesford House
A436
To Stow
④
The Dell
Oddington
Daylesford
③
New Farm
N
500m

driveway which we follow for a short distance, admiring the wonderful views to the right across the parkland. Before reaching a gate across the drive, we are signed to turn left, along a track between fenced fields probably containing horses. This track bends to the right to reach a stone bridge over a dried up stream and keep ahead along the tree lined avenue. At a cross tracks another avenue of trees extends to the left, and private driveway with a horse's head sculpture is to the right, but we keep straight ahead.

Horses head sculpture at entry to parkland

2. Reach the very smart buildings of Daylesford Hill Farm - with an indoor horse exercise area. Go on past the buildings. A path keeps straight ahead, but once beyond the main buildings turn right, signed to The Gardens. Pass the Estate office on our right and walk away from the stud along the surfaced driveway between fields to reach a large wall and buildings on our right. A house with greenhouses is located behind a large wall on the right. The track bends right to follow this wall, and descends slightly, and a gap in the wall reveals a small orchard, and other trees, as well as an inner walled garden. Pass an open field to the left, with lavender and wild flowers, and then a wood on the right. The wood is mainly deciduous, but with some evergreen box. Descend to the level area (may be muddy) and walk on between a field on the left and parkland on the right. Reach a wooden gate and narrow road. Turn right, between hedges - there are no stone walls around here. Pass Daylesford Farm Shop on the left, with its wonderful selection of foodstuffs - at a price. The rooftops of Daylesford come into view as we reach a footpath at a small gate on our left. This is our onward route but first walk on to visit the village with its selection of delightful stone houses, all part of the estate. On the right is the driveway winding away to Daylesford House. This was the home of Warren Hastings, which he acquired in 1788. He remodelled the

mansion in the design of Samuel Pepys Cockerell. On the left is St Peter's church and just beyond that is the old school. The church has a memorial to Charles Edward Baring Young of Daylesford, founder of Kingham Hill Homes for Boys, and also a memorial urn to Warren Hastings in the churchyard. Warren Hastings was the former Viceroy of India who was impeached, but after a seven year trial managed to clear his name.

Warren Hastings memorial urn

3. Retrace steps for 100 yards to a wooden kissing gate where we turn right and walk along the edge of the field to a kissing gate and on to the bridge over the railway – the main Worcester to Oxford line. Over to the right can be seen the former rectory, at the back of the church. Cross the railway line, follow the surfaced track down to a tiny stream (the River Evenlode) and over the bridge, with its impressive iron sides. After a further 100 yards along the surfaced track, go right through a wooden gate and immediately left alongside the hedge. At the end of this field go left through a metal gate back onto the surfaced track, and a few yards along here turn right into the next field. Walk alongside the hedge on the right and at the end of the field turn left, still alongside a hedge, to reach a small patch of woodland and in the corner of the field is a wooden gate. Go on through the gate and a small wood to reach a track. Turn right along here and walk to the remarkable 12th century church of St Nicholas with its famous wall paintings. Here there is a seat in the churchyard, as well as several old yews and masses of snowdrops in season. The village of Oddington was formerly close to the church, but was abandoned in the 18th century, and a new church was built in 1852.

4. Continue along the driveway, now surfaced, and walk beneath a rookery. A path goes off to the left, but we keep ahead to walk into the village, passing some stone houses including the converted Tithe Barn. At the T-junction our route takes us to the right, but first go left

to look at the newer church of Holy Ascension which was built to replace the old church of St Nicholas.

Leave the village by walking past the Post Office, and a row of stone cottages. Where the road bends left to pass The Fox, notice the large house on the right, Oddington House, dating from about 1600. At the A436 turn towards Chipping Norton and walk along the path on the right side. The road narrows and we cross over to follow the narrow path on the other side of the road, up to the bridge over both the River Evenlode and the railway. Just to the left of this bridge is the location of the famed Adlestrop station. At the narrow road signposted Adlestrop and Evenlode, turn left and almost immediately right follow the footpath sign, through a gate into the parkland. Head straight across the large field to pass along the edge of the cricket pitch. In the left corner of the field is a small kissing gate alongside a larger gate. Cross the small stream, go through the gate and follow the track as it leads up towards the village. To the left of our route for the last 400 yards has been a series of small lakes fed by local springs. Coots, ducks and geese may be seen on these lakes, and sometime a heron comes to fish in here. Pass between St Mary Magdalene church and Adlestrop House, which was formerly the rectory. Walk along the road between some lovely houses and take the left fork past the thatched Post Office to return to the starting point at the village hall.

Not to be missed

The small village of Cornwell, a mile to the east of Daylesford Farm, is a small estate village. The tiny church of St Peter is of Norman origin, but was rebuilt in the 19th century. It contains a 13th century font, and has interesting wooden chandeliers based on a design of Clough Williams-Ellis. Its location is separate from the village, possibly because the Black Death wiped out most of the inhabitants. Cornwell Manor is mentioned in the *Domesday Book*, but the present building dates mainly from the 18th century. Much of the village was rebuilt in the 1930s, financed by a wealthy American who employed the architect Clough Williams-Ellis - more famous for his work at Portmeirion. Many of the houses are of limestone, with stone tiled roofs - and several have gateposts with big ball finials and door canopies. The village hall is the centre piece of the village.

St Nicholas church

The oldest parts of the church are the south aisle and the chapel (originally the nave and chancel). The earliest paintings are in the South

Chapel and possibly date from 1250-1275, but the most remarkable feature is the 14th century Doom Painting. Situated on the north wall of the nave, this is possibly the finest version of the Last Judgement to have survived anywhere in England. Doom paintings are pictures of what medieval people thought of heaven and hell, and were used to remind people of the after-life and judgement. After 1860 the church was neglected and became derelict, and although some restoration work began in 1912, the main work was completed beween 1969 and 1974.

Walk 8
Bourton-on-the-Water

This gentle stroll from Bourton-on-the-Water crosses glorious countryside, and takes us alongside the Rivers Windrush and Eye as well as visiting the beautiful stone village of Lower Slaughter before returning to Bourton with its limitless attractions.

Starting point	**The second car park: grid reference 1702203**
Maps	**OS Landranger 163; Explorer OL45**
How to get there	**From the A429 Cirencester to Stow road turn right along Station Road into Bourton. Pass a large car park behind the Texaco garage but drive on into the village and turn left towards Birdland where there is another large car park**
Distance	**4.5 miles**
Time	**About 2 hours, plus any time spent in Bourton or Lower Slaughter**
Terrain	**Level or gently undulating, and mostly on firm clear paths**
Refreshments	**In Lower Slaughter or a huge choice in Bourton**
Nearest (TIC)	**Stow-on-the-Wold (01451 870150) and the independently run centre in Bourton (01451 820211)**

Bourton-on-the-Water, one of the Cotswolds great honey pots, is noted for its stream and small bridges which have given rise to its name of Little Venice, but there is much more besides. The Norman church of St Lawrence had been built on the site of a Saxon building, but was itself demolished in 1784. The present church was built in the 19th century, incorporating a few older parts including the 14th century chancel and Georgian tower. Many old buildings can be seen in the village but it is the bridges which are the most famous feature, with Paynes Bridge leading to Birdland dating from 1776 and the narrow bridge by Victoria Hall from 1756. Bourton is an old village, having existed for at least 6000 years, and has the remains of an Iron age settlement at Salmonsbury on the north eastern edge of the built up area, close to the lakes. The site of the fort covers 24 hectares but has been reduced by ploughing. More modern attractions in Bourton include the model village, a one-ninth scale replica of the real village, and made of local Cotswold stone. At its best in summer, Bourton is a popular tourist attraction all year, and has a special display of Christmas lights, including a tree on a small island in the Windrush. The river is also the site of another attraction, when a traditional football match takes place in the water, during the summer.

The walk

1. From the car park walk through the village, passing the Dragonfly Maze, and then Birdland. The Model Village is on the right, behind the

Bourton on the Water main street

Old New Inn. Continue alongside the stream to walk through the village on High Street, which enables us to see the variety of attractions and numerous locations for refreshment if required. Look out for the Motor Museum, Tourist Information Centre and The War Memorial to the left and the Model Railway Exhibition and church of St Lawrence to our right. As we leave the village, the river is still on our left, with a row of willow trees lining the roadside. At the main road A429, go straight across to a metal gate to take the path signed Public Bridleway and Windrush Way. The Windrush Way is a 13 mile route from Bourton-on-the-Water to Winchcombe, following the high ground of the open wolds. The Wardens' Way also links Bourton-on-the-Water to Winchcombe, via a lower route through the Slaughters. The path is fenced, with the river to our left, and fields stretching away to our right, towards a stone wall and the old railway line. At the end of this field go through the iron gate and move slightly away from the river, and next reach a wooden gate, and move onto the embankment and line of the old railway. This was part of the through route from Cheltenham to Banbury which opened in 1887, though the branch line had reached Bourton in 1862. Traffic on the line declined after 1945, and it was closed in 1962. Our path is shown by an arrow with a blue W, and leads us through a few trees, with open fields to our right. After a few yards on the route of the old railway line, fork right to walk along the field margin, with trees to our left.

2. At a small paddock is a driveway going left to the delightful stone buildings of Aston Farm and Mill, all modernised and in good state of repair. But we turn right alongside the paddock, following the blue arrow and the Gloucestershire Way sign. The path is between lines of trees, and rises gently with open fields on both sides. Reach a gate and an open field with a hedge on the right (though there are also stone walls round some of the fields near here). Pass through a large metal gate and after about 50 yards the path divides. The main track goes straight ahead but we fork right through the hedge, along Macmillan Way. (This is a 290 miles long path across the rolling English countryside from Boston in Lincolnshire to Abbotsbury in Dorset.) Our path leads diagonally to the far corner of the field, to a small metal gate. Cross the road and go straight ahead along a footpath between wire fences. After a slight climb the path begins to descends to reach a minor road linking Bourton-on-the-Water with Upper Slaughter. We keep straight ahead along the narrow road and down to the village. At

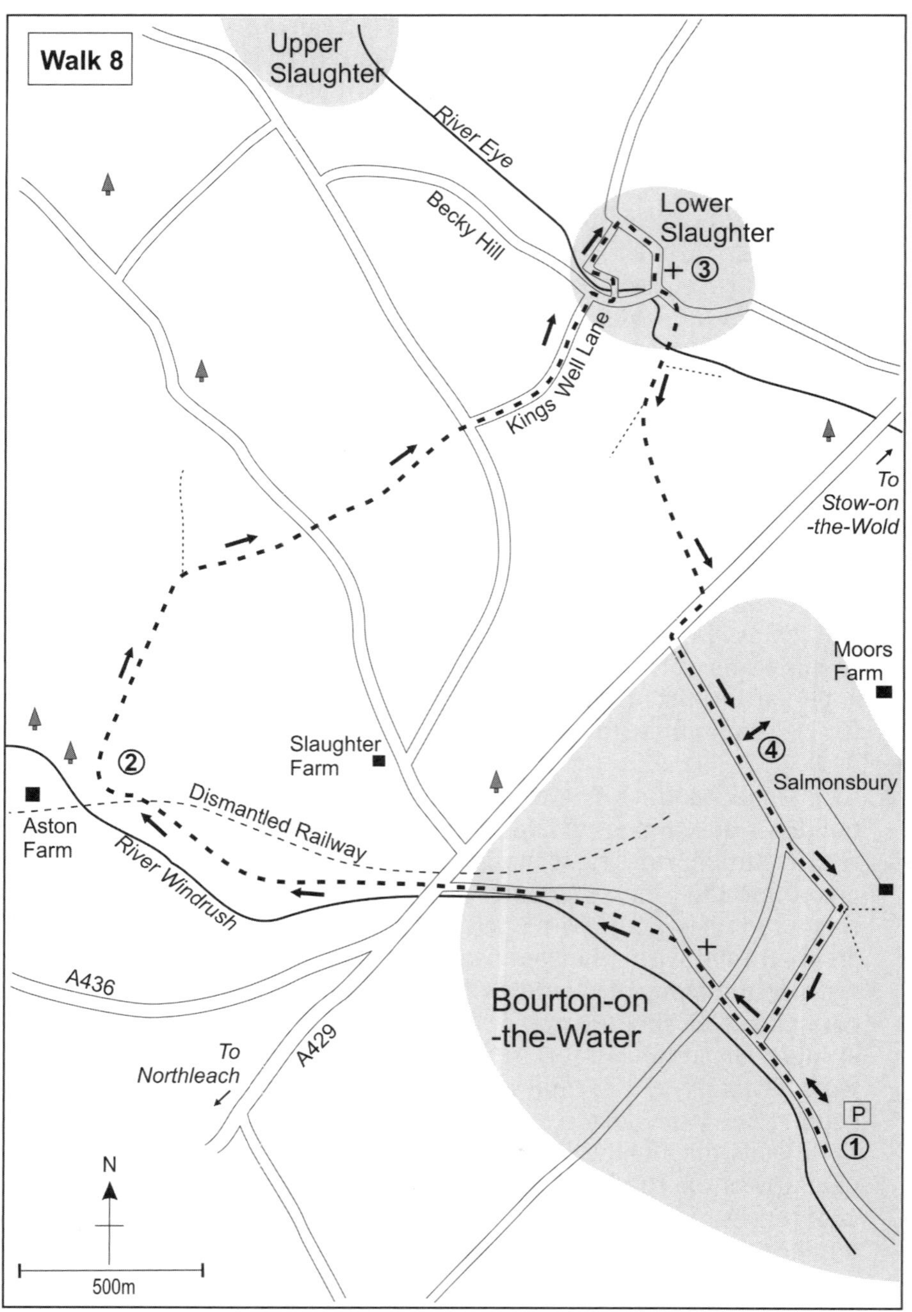

Walk 8
Upper Slaughter
River Eye
Becky Hill
Lower Slaughter
3
Kings Well Lane
To Stow-on-the-Wold
Moors Farm
4
Salmonsbury
Slaughter Farm
2
Aston Farm
Dismantled Railway
River Windrush
A436
Bourton-on-the-Water
A429
To Northleach
P
1
N
500m

the T-junction cross the footbridge over the stream – the River Eye. To the right is a line of beautiful cottages built of the attractive yellowish honey coloured stone, but we turn left to walk round to the mill.

3. The Old Mill is early 19th century and was originally a corn mill. The tall brick chimney was built when steam power was added to the power provided by the waterwheel. The mill is now a shop and museum, open throughout the year.

   Pass the mill, ignore the turning left along Wardens' Way and keep straight ahead. This road leads between stone houses to a T-junction where we turn right between more houses and gardens to walk along towards the church – the spire will soon come into view. The church of St Mary was rebuilt in 1867, in Early English and Decorated styles, by the architect Benjamin Ferrey. The small tower of the previous church was replaced by a tall spire, in slightly different stone. Outside the north east side of the churchyard is a large, 16th century dovecote, believed to have contained as many as 1000 birds. Adjacent to the dovecote is the 17th century manor house, owned by the Whitmore

Old mill wheel in Lower Slaughter

family until 1964. Many alterations have been made, but much of the interior has survived.

Turn left passing the church – and notice on our right the line of cottages we saw earlier, lining the Slaughter Brook (or River Eye) which runs through the village.

The recently rebuilt and refurbished Washbourne hotel is also on the right, in its spacious riverside setting. Formerly cottages and a stable block which were converted into one large private house, this became a cramming preparatory school for Eton, hence the naming of the Scholar's Lounge and the Eton Restaurant. After the floods of July 2007 Washbourne Court was closed for several months whilst undergoing refurbishment. A few yards further along the road is Lower Slaughter Manor Country House Hotel and restaurant on the left, and we turn right here, opposite the gateway to this hotel, and walk alongside the stream. Follow the signs Public Bridleway, Bourton-on-the-Water and Wardens' Way. It is also the Heart of England Way (a 100 mile path which links the Cotswold Way to the Staffordshire Way). Walk alongside the river and keep straight ahead along the path. When this divides, fork left, still on the surfaced path – following the sign for Wardens' Way and to Bourton-on-the-Water. This leads to the main road A429, Fosse Way, and the route of an old Roman Road. To the left can be seen the Coach and Horses, but we turn right as far as the traffic lights, where we turn left along Station Road. Pass the school and hospital on the right and Countryside Stores on the left, and nearly opposite the large car park and Texaco, on the left is Greystone Lane.

4. If wishing to visit the Nature Reserve turn left here, and walk along the narrow road as far as it leads, and arrive at Greystone Farm. But to complete the walk continue along the road to where it reaches High Street, and turn left to retrace steps to the starting point.

Not to be missed

Upper Slaughter is just a mile away from Lower Slaughter, and is another delightful stone village. St Peter's church is a Norman foundation, but has been much changed by restoration and rebuilding work, especially in 1877. The tomb of Reverend Francis Edward Witts, the well-known diarist is here (he wrote the *Diary of a Country Parson*) as he was Rector and also Lord of the Manor. There are monuments to John Slaughter from the 16th century. The church is on a small hill, close to the Norman castle mound, which is just east of the church. Central to the village is The Square, surrounded by eight cottages which were remodelled by Sir Edward Lutyens about 1906. The Lords of the Manor Hotel dates from 1680, and there is also a manor house, at the downstream edge of the village, which was built by the Slaughter family in the 16th century. The name slaughter is thought to have been derived from the Old English word *slohtre* meaning a pool of water or a muddy area.

Greystone Farm Nature Reserve is along Greystones Lane, half a mile from the Texaco garage and one of Bourton's main car parks. This is still a working farm and around the farm buildings geophysical and archaeological surveys have revealed evidence of inhabitants from the Neolithic and Roman periods. Much of the land is now managed for Conservation purposes, and there is an archaeological trail round the remnants of the Iron Age fort. The area has been farmed for 6000 years and the many footpaths enable visitors to cross much of the land, including the Salmonsbury Meadows, now an SSSI (Site of Special Scientific Interest). In addition to the flowers, wild life includes water voles and otters as well as many birds, with summer visitors such as the sedge warbler and winter visiting ducks.

Walk 9
Seven Springs – Coberley circuit

Within a few miles of Cheltenham we walk from the clear and sparkling springs which feed the Thames, to cross rolling countryside and pass through the small villages of Upper Coberley and Coberley. Between these two villages are the sites of the now deserted former medieval villages.

Starting point	**South of Cheltenham close to the junction of A435 and A436. Park in the layby close to the springs, or in the pub car park (with permission). Grid reference 967170**
Maps	**OS Landranger 163; Explorer 179**
How to get there	**Along the A435 south of Cheltenham, or from junction 11A on the M5 along the A417 and then the A436**
Distance	**4.5 miles**
Time	**About 2 hours**
Terrain	**Undulating but with no steep climbs, along tracks, narrow roads and across several fields**
Refreshments	**Nothing along the route, but the Hungry Horse (01242 870219) a Greene King pub at the starting point**
Nearest (TIC)	**Cheltenham (phone 01242 522878)**

The Walk

1. Start from the car parking layby at Seven Springs, which according to many, is the source of the River Thames, but at first, it is called the River Churn. Walk down the steps to the small pool, where you can see the seven springs trickling water into the small pool, from where water

of the infant river flows away into a tunnel beneath the main road. Above this tunnel is a plaque in the wall.

Hic tuus
O tamesina
Septemceminus fons

Which means 'Here O Father Thames is your sevenfold spring'

Walk along the roadside with the Hungry Horse pub on the right, to reach the large crossroads with the A436 and A437. Use the crossing for pedestrians and horses to reach the route of our walk.

Our route is along the track, signed Restricted Byway. Go through the large iron gate and out into the open fields. The track is fenced on both sides and we soon begin to climb steadily through the trees. Emerge at the top of the slope with good expansive views over the surrounding rolling countryside. Many pheasants are bred around here, and in spring and summer skylarks will be singing in the open fields. We reach a narrow road and keep ahead, to pass the route of Gloucestershire Way going to the left. The road divides, by a stone house, and we fork right signed to Upper Coberley, which is a small hamlet. On the right we reach a new dry stone wall and a group of modernised buildings including a smart barn conversion with a wonderful Cotswold stone roof. The medieval village is now away to our right, but nothing remains to be seen.

2. The road descends a little and we pass Lower Farm. Ignore the path which goes off to the left and then as the road bends left, we keep straight ahead along a broad track going off to the right, with some buildings a few yards to the right. Follow the sign for Gloucestershire Way (which extends 100 miles from the Forest of Dean to the Cotswolds) and Public Bridleway, descending steadily through beech trees some of which have been planted in rows. Then reach an area of larch and a straight avenue leading to the edge of the woodland and emerge into an open field. Walk on straight across the middle of a large field and then cross the road and proceed over a stile. In this next field head towards the woods on the far side but veer slightly right to aim towards a large wooden gate. Through here we pass to the left of a small pond and after a few yards reach another gate. Go over a stile to the left of the gate, and proceed along the right side of the next field to another stile, and keep ahead along the edge of the field, with the

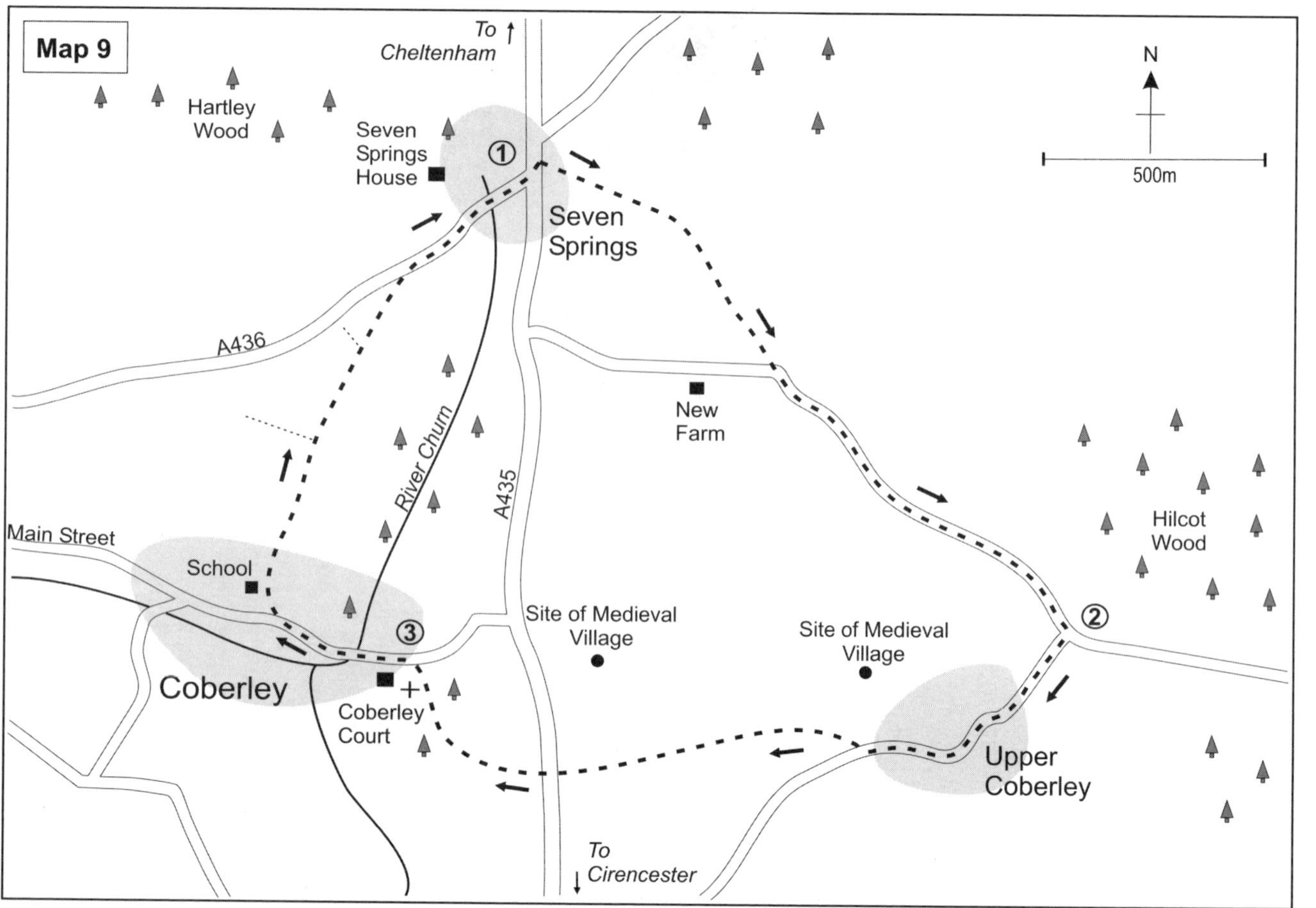

Map 9
To Cheltenham
Hartley Wood
Seven Springs House
①
Seven Springs
N
500m
A436
New Farm
River Churn
A435
Hilcot Wood
Main Street
School
③
Coberley
Coberley Court
Site of Medieval Village
Site of Medieval Village
②
Upper Coberley
To Cirencester

barn and church to the left. Turn left along the narrow road and after a few yards go left through the wooden door in the wall, which leads us through to a large private garden and the churchyard.

3. On the path leading round to the church doorway pass the memorial stone to Lombard, the favourite horse of Sir Giles Berkeley. The large wall here is the wall of the former Coberley Hall, which was removed in the 18th century. It was the home of the Berkeleys, and also for a time the home of Dick Whittington - before he moved to London. His mother was the wife of Sir Thomas Berkeley who fought at the Battle of Crecy. After Sir Thomas died in 1350, she married William Whittington, and a son Richard was born in 1359. He subsequently became Sir Richard and was the Lord Mayor of London. Also on our left just before reaching the church door notice the carved heads on the gravestones and beyond there is the remnant of an old stone cross. The stained glass in the porch is a memorial to a former church warden.

Gravestone with carved heads

The parish church of St Giles dates from the 12th century, and few Norman fragments have survived, but here was a major rebuild of nave and chancel by John Middleton from 1869-72. The South Chapel, was built in 1340 by Sir Thomas Berkeley, and like the tower and porch, was not changed at the rebuild. Inside the church is a fine east window with stone carving beneath. Several impressive tombs include memorials to the Berkeleys in the South Chapel, with Lord Berkeley and Lady Berkeley as well as a child, possibly a daughter, with feet resting on a dog. Other features of interest include the carved font, a 17th century communion table and the unusual heart memorial in the Sanctuary.

Return to the road and continue the walk, to pass over the small River Churn. The road bends left past the Old Post Office, but we fork right, past the No Through Road sign, pointing to the School. Pass the stone column on the small green, and then reach the school. When the road bends left to a row of houses, keep straight ahead along the footpath between hedges – signed to Seven Springs 1 km. We walk along the path which is situated in a sunken lane, and has a stony base, the relic of a former track. Climb steadily for a time, then level off, and as we begin to descend the traffic can be seen ahead on the main road A436. Stay close to the right side of the field and reach a stile going right. Climb over this and continue along the right margin of the field close to a wire fence. Go through a metal kissing gate out onto the road, and follow the narrow verge – take care on this busy road – to return to our starting point. Sandford Special School is over to our left, in the old Seven Springs House and other additional buildings.

Source of the Thames at Seven Springs?

Not to be missed

Seven Springs

In this layby is the source of the Thames, although here it is named the River Churn. This headstream of the Thames flows through Coberley, past

Rendcomb and Cirencester, then Cerney Wick and South Cerney to join the Thames just downstream of Cricklade Bridge. The length of the River Thames is said to be 215 miles (346 km) but this is if measured from the seasonal spring at Trewsbury Mead - at a height of 356 ft (108m) and the precise location varies slightly (see Walk number 19). If the source of the Thames is taken to be at Seven Springs this would add a further 14 miles (22km) to the total length and this would be a permanent flow. The two main arguments in favour of Seven Springs are that the height of the source is higher (just above 700 feet above sea level), and the greater length of the headstream.

Roman Villa at Great Witcombe

Access to Witcombe is from Junction 11A on the M5 along the A417 towards the Cotswolds. After about one mile turn right along the A46 towards Stroud. At the first small roundabout on this road turn left signed to Witcombe. After a quarter mile at the first turning on the right, turn along a narrow road with No Through Road and Roman Villa signs. This leads to a small car park, and then a 300 yard walk along the driveway. Just before Cooper's Hill Farm fork left along the clear footpath which leads to the Villa, on a beautiful site where the natural springs would provide a water supply. The Information Board tells us that this Roman Country House was on a Nobleman's Country Estate situated on a slope and therefore built on terraces, with four different levels. The site was possibly used from the late 1st century AD, though the ruins of buildings which remain date from 250 AD and were used until the 5th century. Heated baths and exercise rooms were included in this spacious villa, and there are remains of a temple shrine for a water spirit.

Walk 10
Sherborne Park and Village

The walk crosses the fields of the productive farmland of the Sherborne Estate and takes us through areas of mixed woodland. The estate contains a wealth of wildlife, especially the spring flowers but also a wide range of birds, fallow and roe deer and several species of bats which live in the caves and tunnels of the former quarries.

Starting point	**National Trust car park at grid reference 158143**
Maps	**OS Landranger 163; Explorer OL 45**
How to get there	**Travel along A40 from Burford towards Cheltenham, and where the left turn leads to Lodge Park we turn right towards Sherborne and a car park. After about 600 yards turn right along the narrow driveway to the National Trust Car park at Ewe Pen (£1 payment requested)**
Distance	**4 miles**
Time	**About 2 hours of comfortable walking. An extra 2 miles is possible if wishing to walk round the water meadows**
Terrain	**Gentle descent to the village and then gentle climb back, but mostly level walking along clear paths. Patches can be muddy in wet weather. No stiles**
Refreshments	**Choice of pubs in Northleach; mall tea shop in Sherborne; Snacks available at Lodge Park when it is open**
Nearest TIC	**Burford (01993 823558)**

The walk

1. The car park is adjacent to the old Cotswold Stone Barn, built around 1860, and used for storing hay and straw and used for bedding and feeding the sheep in the winter – hence the name Ewe Pen. In the 16th century the sheep were washed every year in Sherborne Brook, before going to market. Wool was a great luxury in those days, and that is how Thomas Dutton became so wealthy. Leave the car park and turn right along the driveway. At the end of the long low stone buildings the drive bends slightly right but we take the left fork along the grassy path. Turn left at the end of this field, still staying close to the field margin. Descend slightly as the church spire and part of the village come into view. The path leads into a wood, passing the wooden carving of a shepherd, the first of the sculptures to be passed on this walk. The sculptures were created by local artists, and local school children were involved in the designs. Pass through an area of larch and then deciduous trees to reach a clearing with the metal sculpture of a lifelike deer. The path leads on downhill and divides, where we take the right fork through beech trees and continue down to reach a gap in the wall, and the road.

Metal deer sculpture

Turn right here, to walk through the village, a linear settlement built along the valley of Sherborne Brook, a tributary of the Windrush. The village is in two parts, separated by the grand house and church in the middle. Old stone houses on our left date from 17th, 18th and 19th centuries, and on our right is the open parkland of the estate. Pass Bourton Lodge on our right and then the main drive to Sherborne House – with prominent Private notice. Enjoy the delightful views down to the left to the Sherborne Brook which has been dammed to create small lakes, very popular for wild birds – ducks, swans, geese and gulls.

Sherborne brook and weir

The entrance to the church is on our right - and well worth a visit. St Mary Magdalene probably dates from late 13th century - a previous church probably having been at the eastern end of the village, where fragments can still be seen, in the house number 88. The tower dates from the 14th century, and may have been part of a monastery. Much of the church was rebuilt in the 18th century by James Dutton the first Lord Sherborne, and the second Lord Sherborne made further changes in the 19th century. Major restoration work took place in 1989. The interior contains several impressive memorials to the Dutton family as well as many other features of interest - such as the gilded hanging electric light fittings. A more recent addition to the church is the memorial plaque to James Bradley (1693-1762) who was one of the greatest astronomers of all time. A local boy, born in Sherborne he became the Astronomer Royal but his great claims to fame are his two discoveries concerning the aberration of light and the nutation of the earth's axis - both of which are fundamentals of modern astronomy.

Then we pass the big house, originally built in the 16th century by Thomas Dutton, but having been changed considerably over the centuries. The house is joined to the church by a corridor, but after a spell as a Private School has now been converted into apartments. Next we pass the former stable block - another magnificent building, built for James Dutton in the 18th century - but also now converted into apartments.

2. Pass a Nursery and Garden Centre (noted for Design of Country House Gardens) on the right, then the War Memorial and the Village School, with the former post office on the left, now run as a shop, but which also offers tea. Our return route takes us from the War Memorial to pass behind the church and Sherborne House, but first keep walking ahead along the village street towards the eastern part of Sherborne. The old village pump is on the right and then Stones farm, but on the left are small terraces of 2 or 3 houses, and immaculate gardens.

   Reach a T-junction. For an extension walk, one or two extra miles round the Water Meadows, turn left here along the road and soon reach the signed footpath, showing the route to the River Windrush and the water meadows. These water meadows were first created in 1844 by using sluices and ditches, mainly in order to produce large amounts of grass for sheep and cattle. The water meadows were restored in the early 1990s and are now rich in wildlife including wading birds, dragon flies, water vole and wild flowers.

   But for our onward route we are turning right for a short distance. Follow the road to the right for just over 100 yards to where the road bends left, and on the left side close to the road junction is number 88. This amazing house has incorporated a remnant of an old Norman church and above the 12th century front door is a carved tympanum and zig-zag carving.

3. Now retrace steps to walk back through the village, as far as the War Memorial at point 2. Here is a left turn along the narrow road signed Restricted Byway, which we ignore, but as the village street bends slightly to the right, we keep straight ahead through a gateway in the stone wall, a few yards to the right of the telephone box - and signed with the purple arrow. The path leads through into the trees, with a section of old ha-ha and then large open field on our left. Here, as

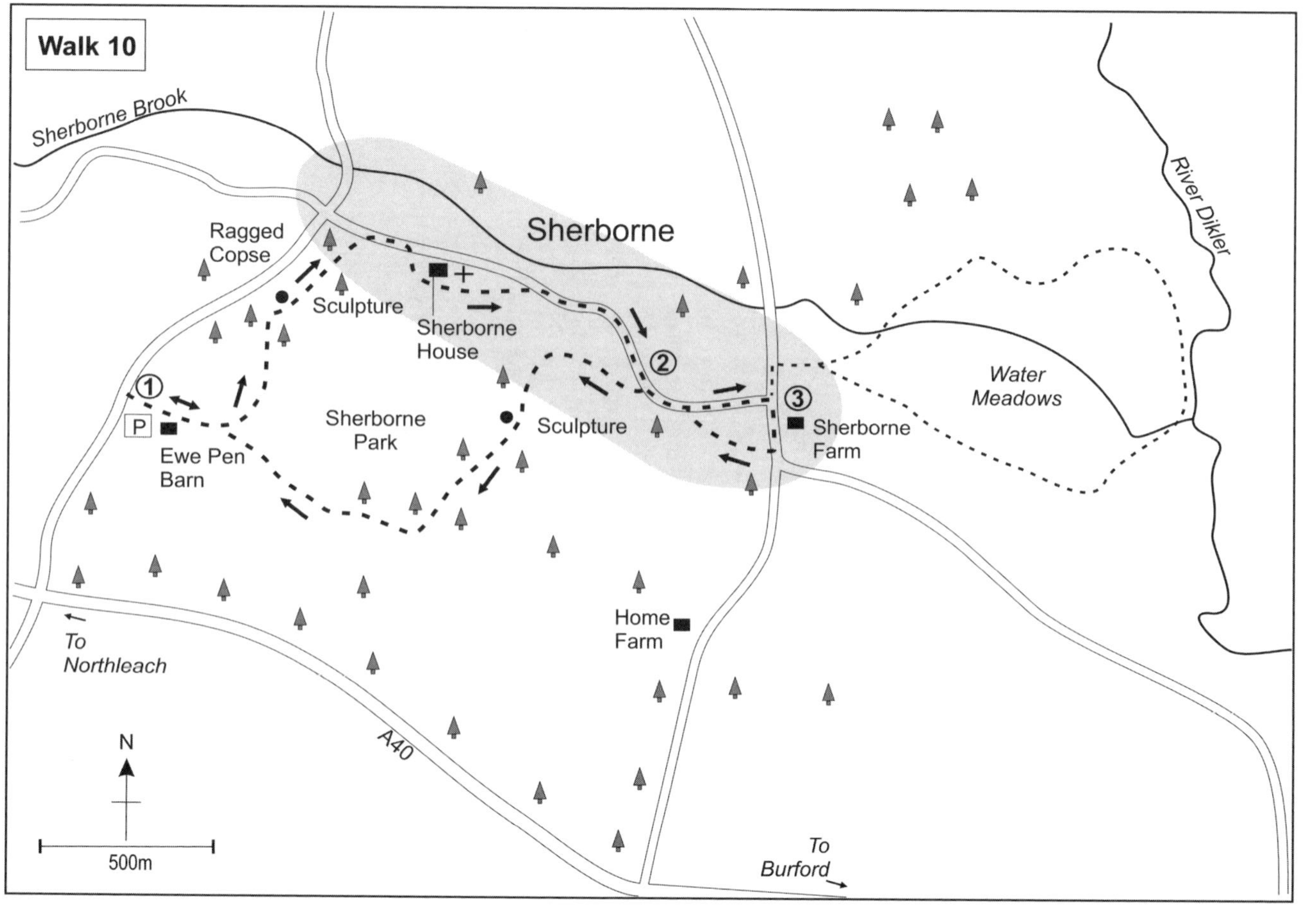
Walk 10
Sherborne Brook
Sherborne
River Dikler
Ragged Copse
Sculpture
Sherborne House
1
2
3
P
Ewe Pen Barn
Sherborne Park
Sculpture
Sherborne Farm
Water Meadows
Home Farm
To Northleach
A40
N
500m
To Burford

elsewhere on this walk are wooden benches for resting or snacking if required – or merely contemplating and looking at the wildlife. The path leads along the back of the church and the big house, with gardens and tennis court. Follow the path along the margin of the open field, to reach another wooden sculpture on a massive old beech tree. Although partially damaged this can still be seen as the life cycle of a stag beetle. The path is signed with purple and blue arrows, and leads into the woods which contain some very old trees. Wild flowers and bird noises are abundant in spring and early summer. Pass the Round Seat on our right, and merge with another path soon to reach a small iron gate and on our left is the Old Ice House, with a small information board. This house dates from before 1820, and the ice was cut from a nearby pond and stored to provide the big house with ice throughout the summer months. Look overhead near here, to see if you can spot the sculptures of the bats – and it is near here that real bats live in the old quarry tunnels. Pass through the iron gate and continue along the clear path, still following blue and purple arrows. Reach a gate and an open field, where Home Farm can be seen away to our left. But, we turn right, with trees on our right and open field to the left. Reach Beech Avenue leading to the left and either turn here to walk as far as the main road, then turn right and follow the clear path around the edge of the large open field, or just take the straight ahead path which passes the playing field to our left, and leads directly to Ewe Pen and our starting point. This last stretch stays close to an amazing stone wall – and will make you wonder just how many people and how many months or years were required to construct all the walls on the Sherborne Estate.

Not to be missed

Northleach, the nearest town, is an old town, granted a charter by Henry III in 1227, which still holds a weekly market as well as the large annual market near the end of June. Importance increased when it became a staging post on the Gloucester-London road which passed through the centre of the town. The modern town sign, commissioned in 1996, stands in the Square and celebrates some of the Northleach history, with the old mill, a sheep, and cross keys to represent the church of St Peter and St Paul. This church, often referred to as 'The Cathedral of the Cotswolds' is one of the great wool churches. It was mostly rebuilt in the 15th century, thanks in part to the generosity of John Fortey whose wealth had come from trade in wool. Amongst many interesting features are the tall octagonal pillars in the nave, with their concave sides. Also there is a good collection of brasses - mainly of wool merchants. The church clock chimes on the quarters and also plays a carillon (*O worship the King*) every three hours. Northleach is also famous for the museum, Keith Harding's World of Mechanical Music, and at the other end of the town is the Old Prison, built in 1790 as a House of Correction. In 2010 the Old Prison was reopened as the new Discovery Centre for the Cotswold AONB (Area of Outstanding Natural Beauty) with interpretive displays and information on geology, history and landscape. Opening hours are 10-4 on Wednesdays to Sundays from April to October. Entry is free.

The old prison

Lodge Park is on the southern edge of Sherborne Park Estate, and opening times are 11-4 on Fridays, Saturdays and Sundays from March to October (phone 01451 844130). The house is a 17th century grandstand built between 1640 and 1655 by the wealthy John Dutton, a friend of Oliver Cromwell, to provide entertainment for himself and friends with banquets and entertainment, especially gambling. The surrounding park was created to support and control the deer, and the mile long walled enclosure was the site for the chase, with the grandstand overlooking the exciting finale - on which the bets had been made. It was not really built as a house, but mainly as a viewing point for watching the deer coursing by greyhounds - with the balcony at the front of the house for the spectators. The surrounding park was designed by the landscape gardener Charles Bridgeman in the mid 1720s, though little of his planning remains.

Walk 11
Swinbrook, Asthall and Widford

Walking through three stone villages and crossing fields of pasture this circuit provides a gentle tour in the glorious countryside of western Oxfordshire.

Starting point	**Swinbrook near the small village green or in the Swan Inn car park (with permission). Grid reference 282119**
Maps	**On the very edge of OS Landranger 163; Explorer OL45**
How to get there	**From the A40 about two miles east of Burford take the narrow road signed to Swinbrook**
Distance	**5 miles**
Time	**2-3 hours**
Terrain	**Gently undulating across fields and along country lanes**
Refreshments	**Swan Inn Swinbrook (01993 823339); Maytime Inn Asthall (01993 822068)**
Nearest TICs	**Burford (01993 823558) and Witney (01993 775802)**

The walk

1. Cross the road from the Swan and go over the stone slab stile signed to Asthall – three quarters of a mile. Veer away to the left away from the fence, across the middle of the field aiming towards the stone slab stile between two gates. Walk along the margin of the next field, by the stone wall, and when the path divides take the left fork, still with wall and fence on our left. Stay close to the field margin, to reach a

stone stile and the narrow road. Turn right. Away to the left is Kitesbridge Farm, as we walk along the road to the bridge over the River Windrush. Reach a farm and the stone houses of the small village of Asthall - with good views across to the church and Asthall Hall, over to the right. When the road divides take the right fork past the Maytime Inn, freehouse and restaurant, with a large car park.

The attractive stone church of St Nicholas dates from Norman times with ancient font and solid pillars. Several changes have been made through the centuries. It was enlarged in 1160, and the chancel was rebuilt in the 13th century, in Early English style. The tomb of Lady Jane Cornwall, resident of the original Asthall Manor, lies in the north chapel. The bell tower was added in the 15th century and a major restoration took place in 1885. Behind the church is Asthall Manor, parts of which date from 1620. In the early 19th century this was bought by the first Baron Redesdale. Several changes were made, including the installation of electricity from water power on the Windrush in 1899. The Redesdale title became extinct in the 19th century because there were no descendants, but was revived in 1902,

Tomb of Lady Jane Cornwall

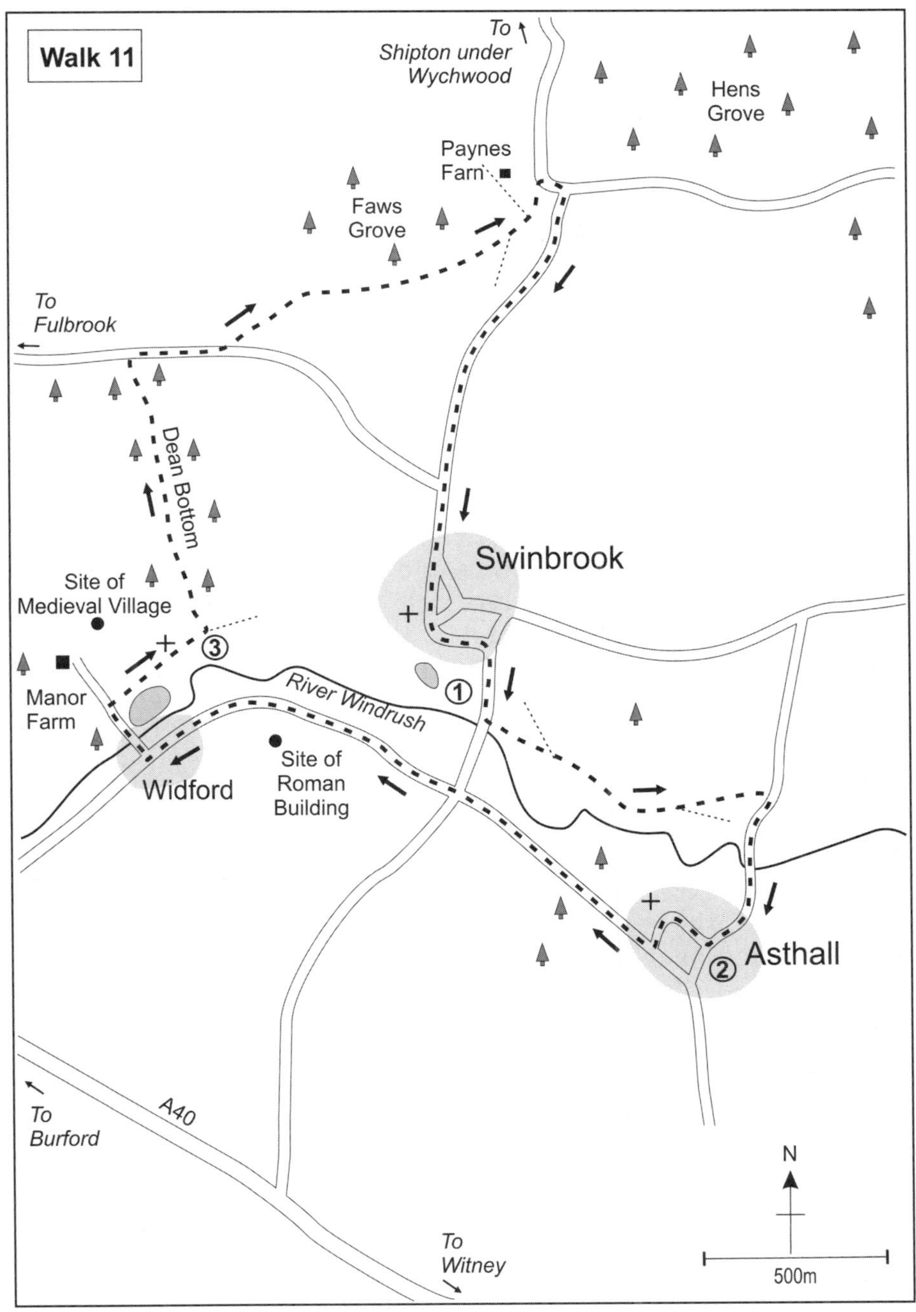
Walk 11
To
Shipton under
Wychwood
Hens
Grove
Paynes
Farm
Faws
Grove
To
Fulbrook
Dean Bottom
Swinbrook
Site of
Medieval Village
3
Manor
Farm
1
River Windrush
Widford
Site of
Roman
Building
2
Asthall
A40
To
Burford
To
Witney
N
500m

when Freeman-Mitfords were raised to the peerage. In 1916 the house was altered by Bateman for the 2nd Lord Redesdale, father of the Mitford girls, and the family lived here until 1926 when they moved to a new house Lord Redesdale built in Swinbrook. Deborah, the youngest daughter was born at Asthall.

Walk on beyond the church, following the road. At the T-junction note the fine avenue of trees to the left, but we turn right, passing the gateway to Asthall Manor, with Anthony Turner's solid sculptures on top of the gateposts. In the garden is an exhibition of modern sculptures, and the gardens have been redesigned by Julian and Isobel Bannerman in 1998.

2. Follow this country lane for about a mile, the first half being very straight as far as the crossroads, where Swinbrook and our starting point is a few hundred yards to the right. Keep straight ahead, with the river, and the cricket pitch, on our right. Remains of a Roman building have been found in a field to the left. We reach Widford Mill Farm on the right, and then turn right along the narrow road, signed to Widford (the name meaning the ford by the willows). Pass the mill, originally for fulling and later for paper, and Mill Race House, then cross over the river. The road climbs up to the few houses of the village, but before the slope begins, turn right along a clear track with a footpath sign to Swinbrook. Pass a small lake on the right as we walk towards the small chapel. Divert from the track to visit the isolated chapel. Evidence of the abandoned medieval village can be seen in several fields nearby. The chapel is named after St Oswald possibly because his body was brought here on his way from Lindisfarne to Gloucester. The church belonged to St Oswald's Priory in Gloucester. Much of the building dates from 12th and 13th century but the lower part of the walls and the blocked north doorway may be earlier. The tub font is early 13th century; the windows 16th and 17th century; and box pews 18th or 19th century - probably made by local carpenters from the Fettiplace Estate. A mosaic pavement which was part of a Roman villa was discovered in the 1904 restoration, but is at present concealed to protect it from vandalism. Paintings on the north chancel wall possibly date from 1350.

3. From the chapel retrace down to the track and continue towards the lone house where the path divides, straight on to Swinbrook, but we

View across to the Chapel of St Oswald

turn left at the marker post. Head towards the valley and reach a strange wooden stile alongside a large wooden gate. Keep ahead up the dry valley, Dean Bottom, with narrow woodland on both sides. As we climb, the woods close in and the valley bends slightly. Walk on up to a stile and a narrow road. Turn right here for about 300 yards then fork left along the broad track, a Restricted Byway, between hedges. Drop down slightly to a small metal gate, alongside a larger gate, and keep ahead, climbing up an open grassy path, with a dry valley down to our right. The wood, Faws Grove, on our left, is a remnant of the old Royal Forest of Wychwood. We approach the corner of the wood but just keep ahead to a metal gate and on downhill along the stony track between walls. Reach a narrow road and turn right, going downhill passing a few stone houses. We also pass a duck pond, fed by springs from the hills, and feeding the small stream which flows down the valley to join the Windrush. Follow the road downhill to Swinbrook, passing several stone houses, then a narrow road to the right, before reaching the village. The church is on our right, then the small green and Village Hall to the left. Pass a farm on the left, and a large converted barn, before reaching the Swan.

St Mary's church dates from 1200, and the nave is transitional between Norman and Early English. The pews were given by Lord Redesdale and his brother in 1926, the 18th century chandeliers came from Asthall Manor, a gift of Lady Redesdale. The two trios of reclining figures are the 17th century Fettiplace memorials, and opposite these are five interesting 15th century misericords. Restoration work took place in 1816, 1864, 1897 and last major repairs in 1975. Outside the church can be seen the unusual open-sided bell tower, added in 1822. Close to the church door notice the graves of Nancy, Unity and other members of the Redesdale family including a grave stone for Diana Mosley.

Memorial

Nancy Mitford gravestone in Swinbrook Churchyard

The former Swinbrook Manor, home of the Fettiplace family, was said to be the finest Tudor House in Oxfordshire. This was destroyed in 1806 and few visible remains can be seen except for former dairy, fishponds and formal terraces. A later Swinbrook House was built by Lord Redesdale in the

1920s and the family moved here from Asthall, until 1936 when they sold the house. Some of the daughters did not like living here.

Not to be missed

Burford church

Use the free car park near the River Windrush and the church at the bottom of the main street in Burford. This church is even finer than the three churches seen on the walk.

The church of St John Baptist stands alongside the River Windrush, and gains 5 stars in the Simon Jenkins book of *England's Thousand Best Churches* - one of only 18 in the country. Built from 1175 until completion in 1500 it stands on the site of an earlier church, and contains many features of interest. The decorated west doorway dates from about 1175. Changes in the 13th century turned this into a cruciform church - the fashion of the time. The Norman Font has 14th century carvings of St Mary and St John on either side of the cross. Amongst the historical links are the Harman Memorial to Edward Harman who was Henry VIII's surgeon. The Tanfield Tomb dates from the 17th century. Sir Lawrence Tanfield was James I's Chancellor of the Exchequer. The Epona stone is set high on the south wall. A sculptured stone slab dates from the 12th century or older, possibly even from Roman times. It shows three figures one mounted and two on foot - the Three Disgraces as they used to be called by choirboys. They are most likely 12th century, and showing Mary and Joseph with Jesus on the donkey. In the churchyard too are links with the past, notably the Bale tombs. Shaped like bales of wool, often thought to be associated with the wool merchants, several of whom provided money for the church, but the dates suggest they were much later than the time of the wealthy wool merchants. Another suggestion is that they represent the pall which often covered the hearse.

Also not to be missed is the Wild Life Park just outside Burford, 2 miles south of the junction of the A361 and A40. Not only home for a wide range of animal life but also containing large areas of gardens. Attractions for visitors include rhinos, camels, lions, a tropical house, a lemur enclosure, insect house, and walled garden. There are lawns for picnics, children's farmyard, playground, small narrow gauge railway as well as restaurant. Open daily. Phone 01993 823006.

Walk 12
Chedworth

The route takes us across the open plateau over farmland and a former airfield before walking through the woods and passing the Roman Villa on the return walk to the village.

Starting point	**Grid Reference 052121 in the village at the pub or close to the church (except when services are taking place). An alternative starting point can be at the wide space on the narrow road along the far side of the airfield at grid reference 041132**
Maps	**OS Explorer OL45; Landranger 163**
How to get there	**Turn off the A429 between Northleach and Cirencester; or turn off the A436 near Andoversford and follow the narrow road through Withington to Chedworth**
Distance	**Nearly 5 miles**
Time	**2-3 hours**
Terrain	**Level at first then undulating through the woods, where it can be muddy**
Refreshments	**Seven Tuns in Chedworth (phone 01285 720242) which dates from 1610**
Nearest TICs	**Northleach (01451 860715) and Cirencester (01285 654180)**

Chedworth village

It is worth wandering round this delightful village with its lovely stone houses and colourful gardens. Set in a deep valley, it is surrounded by glorious countryside. Queen Street is named in memory of Elizabeth of York, wife of Henry VII, who in 1491 visited her aunts who lived in the Manor. The church of St Andrew dates from 1100 AD and in spite of a major rebuild in the mid 15th century (financed by profit from sheep farming) and restoration work in 1883, many Norman features can still be seen. These include three Norman arches in the nave, the arch leading to the tower and the tub shaped font. The lower part of the short tower is Norman in origin, although added to later in order to make it higher. Amongst other interesting features inside are the long perpendicular windows, one on each side of the 13th century porch. The wine glass pulpit dates from the 15th century and there is a *Breeches Bible* in a glass case in the north east corner. In use until the Authorised Version was produced in 1611, the Breeches is the collectors term for any copy of the old *Geneva Bible* of 1560. The word breeches is taken from *Genesis* III, Verse 7, 'they sewed fig leaves together and made themselves breeches'. A framed extract from the *Domesday Book* can be seen in a showcase, and on the north wall is the *Virgin and Child* sculpture from 1911, by Helen Rock.

Church of St Andrew

Interesting carving on tomb near church door

The walk

1. Start from near the Seven Tuns pub and walk towards the church of St Andrew, passing a spring with a waterwheel in the garden above. Walk along the narrow path towards the church, passing many carved headstones and tombs. The battlements and gargoyles to be seen on the church wall are from the 15th century. The

path leads on to the left of the church to reach a wooden V-shaped pinch stile. Go straight across this small field to a stone slab stile and on to a driveway. Manor Farm is just to our right and we follow the drive away from the farm, passing the village cricket pitch. Looking back the village will have disappeared from site as it is tucked down in the hollow. At the road turn right along the track, passing behind the cricket pavilion and over a stile to go straight ahead along the track. Pass a small clump of trees on the right and notice the breeding pens for game birds in this small wood. At the end of the drive, go over the stile and on to the old airfield, where remnants of old buildings can be seen. Here is the memorial planting of Clarkes Covert, as we head diagonally right across a wide open field. Reach a stile, with a barn away to our right – but keep straight ahead across an old runway and over another stile. Cross the next field to reach an area of hard standing and another runway. The path divides here but keep ahead, aiming towards the old huts just to the left of a clump of fir trees.

2. Reach a wooden pinch stile and the narrow road – where there is space for parking and an alternative starting point if required. Turn right

Inside Chedworth Roman Villa

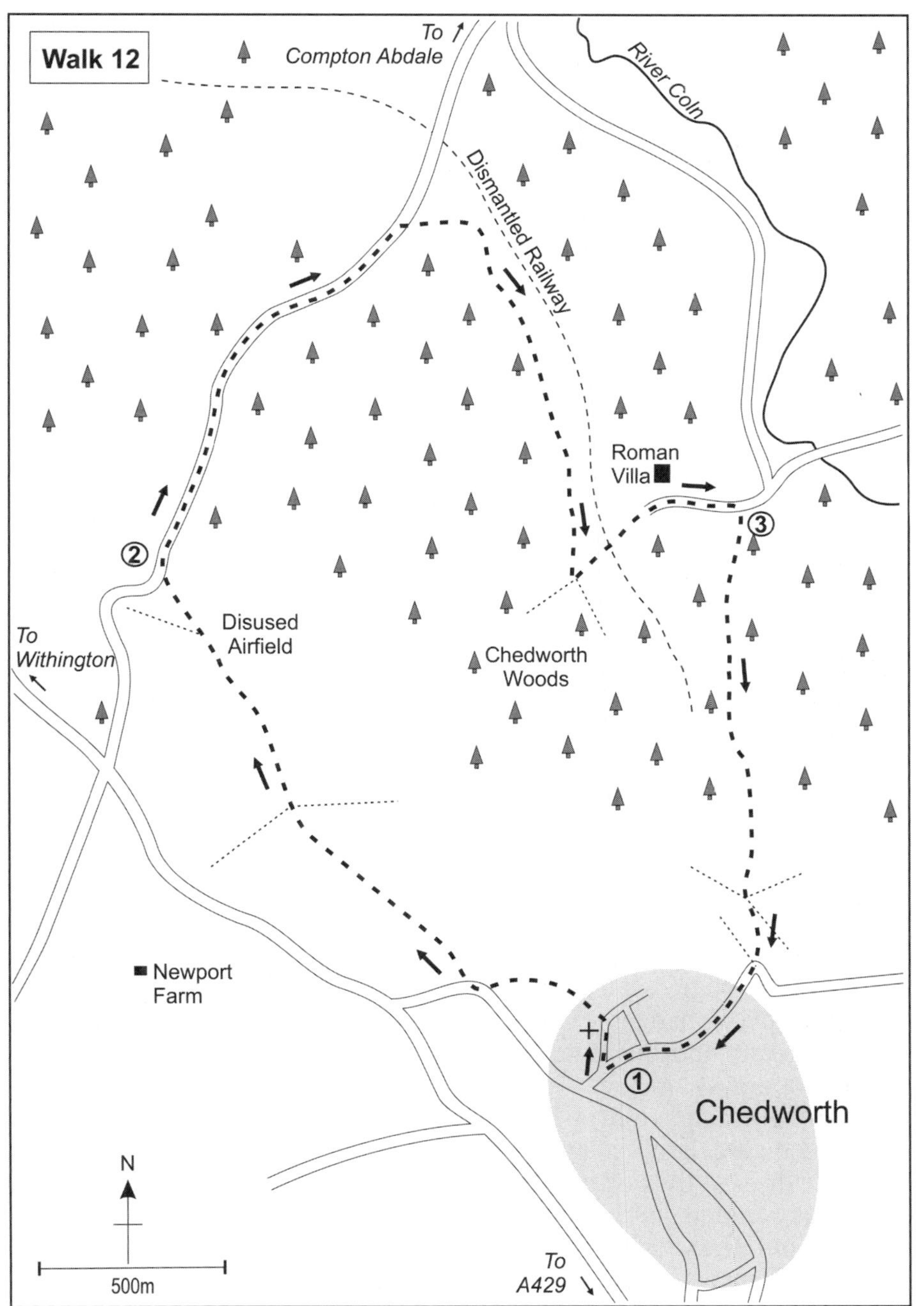
Walk 12
To Compton Abdale
River Coln
Dismantled Railway
Roman Villa
To Withington
Disused Airfield
Chedworth Woods
Newport Farm
Chedworth
N
500m
To A429
②
③
①

along the road which leads through the woods for just over half a mile. Descend quite steeply and then level off as we reach a footpath into the Chedworth woods, where we turn right, through the wooden stile. The clear path descends and bends left at first and then just before reaching a high embankment for the old railway line bend right and begin to climb quite steeply. The woods are of mixed deciduous trees with undergrowth - and containing many spring flowers as well as summer visiting birds and butterflies. The path becomes barer and wider, as we begin to climb. There are signs of former coppicing around here, and some stony areas of the path, evidence of an old trackway. Just beyond an area of fir trees, where there is less undergrowth and fewer wild plants, a stony stretch of path descends steeply to a cross paths, where we turn left - signed to the Villa. Continue to descend and pass beneath the old railway line, to reach the end of a surfaced road, with the Roman Villa on the left. The railway line was a single track route from Cheltenham to Cirencester operated by the Midlands and South West Railway from 1891-1969. The line crossed the Chedworth valley on a viaduct, which has now gone, though embankments can still be seen. The old line is now used as a cycle track.

3. Walk along the road. As it bends left, our path goes to the right - along a stony driveway, which is the entrance to the National Trust car park. This is a bridleway and level at first, crossing an area rich with a profusion of wild flowers, as well as butterflies. Pass beneath a copper beech and begin to climb up the well-made stony track. This is quite sunken in places, as a result of erosion along an old established track. Climb steeply up through the woods. Quite a few beech trees here, as well as noisy birds such as the pheasants and woodpeckers. Emerge at the top of the woods as the slope levels off. The track bends left into an open grassy field, but we keep straight ahead along a narrow path between hedges - still climbing slightly, and following signs for a bridleway and the Monarch's Way. The slope levels off as we walk along a grassy track between fields. At a five-ways junction of paths, take the second right, which is over a small stile alongside a small wooden gate. Drop steeply down a small field with wild flowers and butterflies. At the bottom, by the magnificent stone house, go through a large wooden gate and turn left to walk along the drive - with good views into the village of Chedworth, perched on the valley sides. When the drive meets the narrow road, turn right and walk steeply downhill,

to pass between stone houses and colourful gardens. We cross a tributary of the River Coln and the line of the former railway, and amongst the interesting old stone houses we pass are the Old Bakery and The Buttress. When the road divides fork left between Corner Cottage and Ivy Cottage to walk steeply up the valley side to reach the Seven Tuns.

Not to be missed

Roman Villa

Looked after by the National Trust, the Villa is open from mid March to mid November, from 10-4 (till 5pm in the summer) every day except Mondays. One of the largest Roman Villas in England, it dates from the early 2nd century. The site in this sheltered valley was chosen because of the spring and a reliable water supply, so essential for the bathing which was an important part of Roman social life. However the sloping ground created building problems so some land had to be terraced. The main house was on the west side of the valley and a small baths area was on the north. The earliest villa was not very grand, but additions were made, including mosaics and a larger bath house. The garden court was created early in the 4th century and the house remained occupied until near the end of that century. Many artefacts are on show in the museum. The villa was discovered in 1864 when a gamekeeper noticed that rabbits had dug up a few pieces of mosaic.

Walk 13
Painswick

We walk along narrow roads down to the Painswick Stream and then through pasture meadows before climbing back up towards Painswick Hill where we walk through woods and across the golf course, via the Kimsbury Iron Age Camp on the top of Painswick Beacon.

Starting point	Walkers Car Park, grid reference 867105
Maps	OS Explorer 179; Landranger 162
How to get there	To Painswick along the A46 from Stroud or Cheltenham and from the town centre take the B4073 signed to the Rococo Garden. Opposite the entrance to the garden is the narrow road leading to the free Walkers car park
Distance	about 5.5 miles
Time	Up to 3 hours
Terrain	One downhill stretch early in the walk and later a climb up out of the valley. Paths clear but there may be muddy patches in wet weather
Refreshments	Very good choice of pubs and cafés in Painswick. The Falcon Hotel has a car park at the rear and a very convenient position opposite the church (phone 01452 814222)
Nearest (TIC)	Painswick Town Hall, at present seasonal and manned by volunteers (07503 516924), or in Stroud (01453 760960)

The walk

1. At the car park is a map of the area with comments about Painswick Hill, including a very clear aerial view of the hill fort.

From the walkers car park follow the narrow road, and the Cotswold Way is soon signed forking to the left across the golf course, but we stay along the road, with gardens to the right, and then a short stretch of the golf course. At the cross roads turn right and begin to go downhill to reach the main road the A46. Take care here as the traffic is fast, and we cross straight over signed to The Park and Sheepscombe. The narrow road goes downhill steeply, and when it divides we fork left towards Sheepscombe and Butcher's Arms. A footpath goes left here but we stay on the road and continue downhill past Damsell's Cross. At the bottom of the hill Damsell's Farm is to the left and a footpath signed Wysis Way, the 88km link route between Offa's Dyke Path and the Thames Path. We stay on the road for a few more yards to cross over the river (Painswick Stream) passing the magnificent stone buildings of Damsell's Mill with the date of 1674 over the door.

2. Then we turn left and go over the stile into a field, with the stream on our left. At the end of the field keep straight ahead across the next field to where a small stream trickles across the path as it flows down to join the Painswick Stream. The path divides and we take the left fork to reach a stile and a small patch of woodland. Cross the stream close to the remnants of old building (the ruins of Olivers Mill) and on the right is a Danger Deep Water notice. Then pass the pond on our right and the very attractive isolated house on the left. Reach a large wooden gate and a stile and our path continues along the right margin of the field. Next we approach the group of buildings at Tocknell's Court. Cross over the stile and fork left on to the driveway where we turn right to pass the house with its dovecot and stone gateposts topped by the guardian lions. The stream is on our right as we continue along the drive to reach a narrow road where we turn left.

3. Follow this road as it climbs up the side of the valley, to be joined by the narrow road coming from Cranham and shortly reach the main road. Turn right here along the verge for a few yards and then left on a narrow road to reach a small car parking area and the Cotswold Way. Turn left here and enter Buckholt and Rough Park Woods, parts of the Cotswold Common and Beechwood National Nature Reserves. To the right through the trees can be seen the slope rising to the top of Kites Hill at 253m. Our path leads out of Buckholt Wood and along a narrow road for a few yards to Castle Lodge House where the path divides.

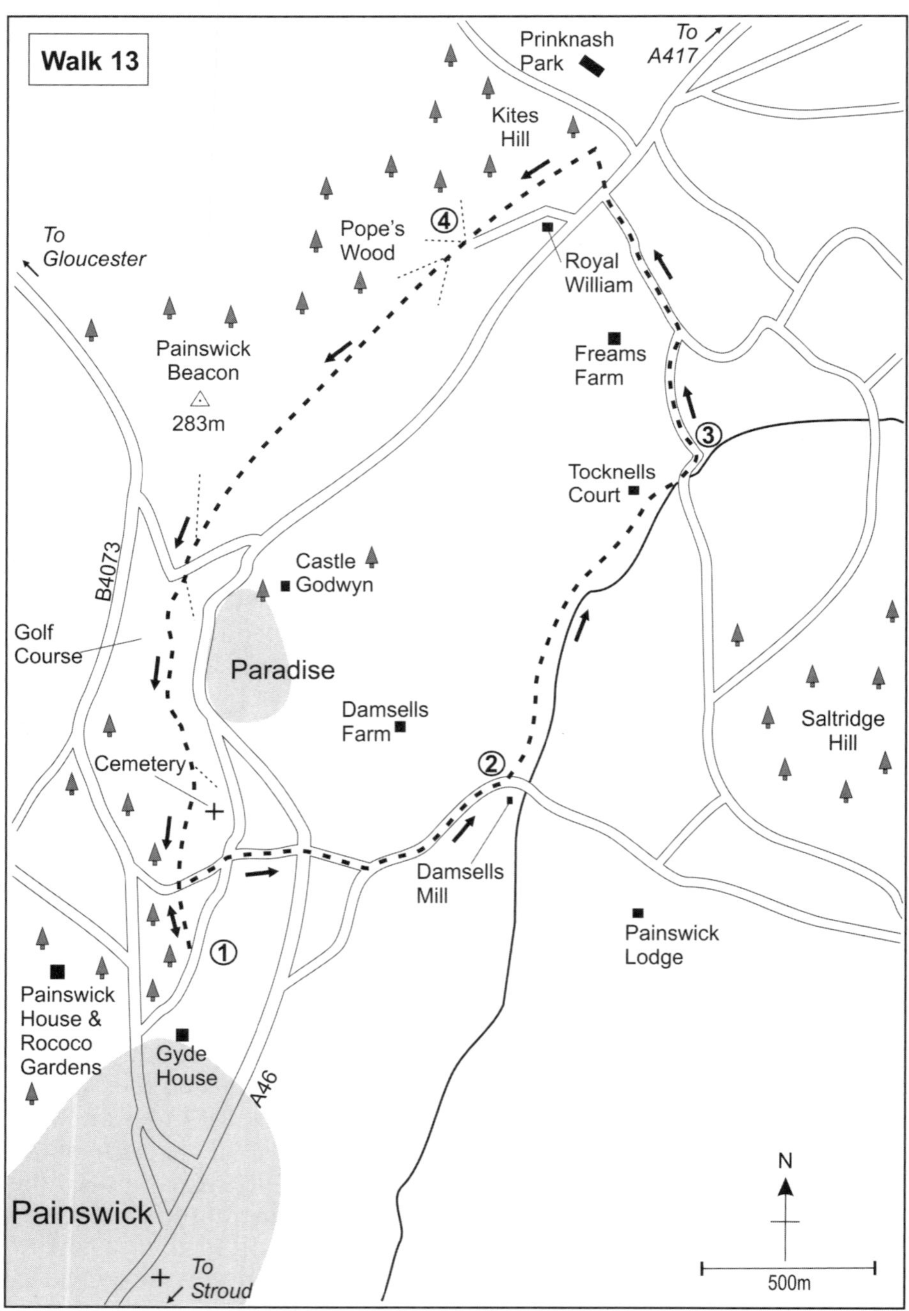

Walk 13
Prinknash Park
To A417
Kites Hill
Pope's Wood
4
Royal William
To Gloucester
Painswick Beacon
283m
Freams Farm
3
Tocknells Court
B4073
Castle Godwyn
Golf Course
Paradise
Damsells Farm
Saltridge Hill
Cemetery
2
Damsells Mill
Painswick Lodge
1
Painswick House & Rococo Gardens
Gyde House
A46
N
Painswick
To Stroud
500m

Pope's Wood is to our right but we keep straight ahead signed the Cotswold Way and Public Bridleway, and emerge onto the edge of the Golf course.

4. This route soon divides and we must make a choice.

Either take the right fork along a stony track which leads to the top of the Beacon and the triangulation point at 283m (928ft) where wonderful views open across to the east, to the Malverns and beyond. From the Beacon keep straight ahead and drop down to the lower area close to another Information Board.

Or, stay on the grassy path undulating across the golf course following the acorn sign, and passing to the left of the Beacon, with the massive embankments running parallel to our path.

On the top of Painswick Hill stands the impressive hill fort of Kimsbury Camp, one of 35 Iron Age Hill forts in Gloucestershire. This multi-vallate camp has deep and steep ditches, with two or three embankments enclosing about seven acres of land, including holes of the golf course. Outer banks are not complete circuits all the way round. The fort may date back to 500 BC and was occupied until about 40 AD.

Both options lead us on to reach a narrow road, where we turn left for about 30 yards. As the road bends left, fork right on the track signed Cotswold Way, and this leads us along the left side of the former

View to village of Paradise

Catbrain quarry, at present used by Heritage Masonry Company, but formerly the source of stone used in the houses of Painswick and also in Gloucester cathedral. The track narrows to a path and we enter the woods, passing a gap in the trees with open views across the valley over the small hamlet of Paradise (thought to have been named by Charles I who stayed near here whilst besieging Gloucester) and the hillside beyond Damsell's Mill. We emerge from the trees and cross part of the golf course. Move slightly right to pass alongside the stone wall which surrounds the trees and the cemetery. Keep straight ahead across more of the golf course and return to the walkers car park.

Not to be missed

Painswick House Rococo Gardens

These gardens were created by Charles Hyett in the 1740s, and taken over by his son Benjamin when Charles died, but later abandoned and over planted with woodland. Lord Dickinson, a descendant of Charles Hyett, inherited Painswick House in 1955, and in 1984 began work on restoring the gardens to their former state. In 1988 he handed control to the Painswick Rococo Garden Trust, with a long lease. There were no records or plans of how the garden had looked in the 18th century, but fortunately Benjamin Hyett had commissioned a local artist Thomas Robins to paint the garden in 1748. This painting provided invaluable information about how the garden had looked. Garden historians were very interested in the period 1720-1760 which became known as the Rococo period. Rococo gardens have walks with vistas and buildings at strategic locations, rather than just concentrating on formal beds of flowers. Opening times are 11-5 daily, from early January until the end of November. Telephone 01452 813204.

The garden is different each year as changes are made but the snowdrops are always outstanding and the interesting buildings such as the Exedra and Red House add to the scenery of the garden. A maze was created in 1998 for the 250th anniversary of the Robins painting.

Painswick

St Mary's church is surrounded by 99 yew trees - now numbered - and local legend says that the devil will never allow the 100th tree to grow, although a yew tree was given to every parish in the Diocese of Gloucester in 2000 to mark the new millennium.

Yew trees in Churchyard

A local rhyme is:

Painswick maidens shall be true
Till there grows the hundredth yew.

Every year in September there is a clypping service when the local children process round the churchyard and form a ring to surround the trees, and then sing a traditional hymn. The word clypping is taken from an old Saxon word meaning embrace, and is not referring to clipping or pruning the trees, although this is done once each year.

The churchyard also contains an outstanding collection of 17th and 18th century table and pedestal tombs, perhaps the finest in England. These were made of local limestone for the wealthy wool merchants in the town. Part of the church dates from 1380, the nave and tower are from 1480-90, and the soaring spire was built in 1632. Amongst many interesting features inside the church is a model of Drake's flagship at the Armada. The ship is an ancient symbol of the Christian church and the word nave is derived from the Latin word for a ship. Just outside the churchyard are the spectacle stocks which date from about 1840.

The Post Office is located in a 15th century building, the oldest building in Britain containing a post office and is the only building in Painswick with exposed timber framing. Several fine old stone buildings in the town have survived and been well maintained, and along Bisley Street, number 16 is the Tudor Byfield House with a large 14th century donkey door, through which donkeys laden with loads of fleeces could pass to the wool barn at the rear. The Chur, number 17, a 14th century house and coffee house, has a studded door which was also a donkey door. Number 18 is owned by the National Trust and was formerly part of the 14th century Fleece Inn.

Walk 14
Bibury

William Morris described Bibury as the most beautiful village in England, and after exploring the village a walk round the surrounding countryside completes a very good day out - and there is a choice of eating places for lunch and tea in the village.

Starting point	Grid reference 114068
Maps	OS Landranger 163; Explorer OL45
How to get there	From Cirencester take the B4425 towards Burford, via Barnsley. Free parking opposite the old mill and the Trout Hatchery, or on the road alongside the River Coln
Distance	5.5 miles but with the southerly extension is about 8 miles
Time	3-4 hours
Terrain	Gently undulating countryside with short steeper stretches uphill when leaving the village, or downhill when returning
Refreshments	Swan Inn (01285 740695) and Catherine Wheel (01285 740250) are both in the village
Nearest TIC	Cirencester (01285 654180)

In the car park a large notice board has information about the Rack Isle, a low lying meadow surrounded by the River Coln and Arlington Mill Stream. The name was obtained because of the wooden racks which were used to stretch woollen cloth produced at Arlington Mill. Rack Isle has been managed by the National Trust since 1956 and everyone is able to enjoy this attractive island, home to birds, plants and animals. Arlington Row stands at the far end. These cottages, built of local stone and with

Looking towards the Swan Hotel

stone roofs, date from c.1380 when they were probably used as a monastic wool store. In the 17th century they were converted into cottages for local weavers who supplied wool to Arlington Mill.

Bibury is an ancient settlement with an Iron Age hill fort nearby, just south of Ablington. The church is ancient too, and has Saxon origins. Two important routeways pass close by, with Akeman Street and the Roman Road from Cirencester to St Albans to the south, and the old Saltway from Droitwich to Lechlade to the north. However, much of the growth and wealth came from association with sheep farming, and in modern times tourism is the major activity - helped by its location and the approval given by William Morris. Across the River Coln is Arlington which joins with Bibury to become one settlement. Also on the River Coln is Ablington the third of the stone villages we see on this walk.

The Walk

1. From the car park opposite the Trout Hatchery, turn left along the road, with the Trout Farm and the old Arlington Mill (formerly a Folk

Museum of Victoriana including old agricultural implements) on the right. The mill dates from the 17th century, and worked cloth at first and later corn. Pass the Old Forge on the left and Mill Cottage, on the right, and an Antique shop. Climb steadily up the main street towards the Catherine Wheel, which dates from the 15th century. Shortly beyond the pub, close to the telephone box turn right along the narrow road with the No Through Road sign. When this road divides take the left fork signed to Ablington. Pass to the left of Arlington Farmhouse and keep straight ahead through a small wooden gate and then over a rock slab stile or through a large gate into a field. Reach another rock slab stile and cross a driveway by a barn. Keep straight ahead through a gate, and then veer away from the fence on our right to cross the middle of the next field, to a kissing gate and stile. Keep straight ahead with a wire fence on our right, to reach a stile and two small gates and continue along a path between fence and hedge to a narrow road by a lone house. Turn right and begin to descend to a road junction. Turn right here and pass the entrance to Ablington Manor, with beautiful gardens (swathes of snowdrops in season).

J. Arthur Gibbs lived in the Elizabethan Ablington Manor, which dates from 1590. He wrote about daily life in his book of 1898, *A Cotswold Village*, which depicted life in Victorian times. One of several small cottages in the village was owned by John Brown, the local gamekeeper and basis of the character Tom Peregrine in the Gibbs book.

Cross over the river and bend to the right. The road soon divides where there is a small bus shelter on the right (with eggs for sale - trust the customer), and we keep straight ahead here to walk out of the village. After about 200 yards reach a slightly bigger road and turn left, uphill. When the road bends to the right, fork right along a stony track, a bridleway, by Hinton Cottage.

2. Climb steadily between fields, to emerge onto the open plateau surface with distant all round views. Keep straight ahead for more than a mile to reach a cross tracks and Saltway Barn. Turn right at the barn, on the track running along the margin of a large field, with the hedge on the right. Reach a pheasant rearing area in a small wood, New Covert Plantation. At the end of the next field, at a cross paths turn right, to walk along a field margin with hedge on our right. Go through a gate and along the track to pass to the left side of the modernised Hale

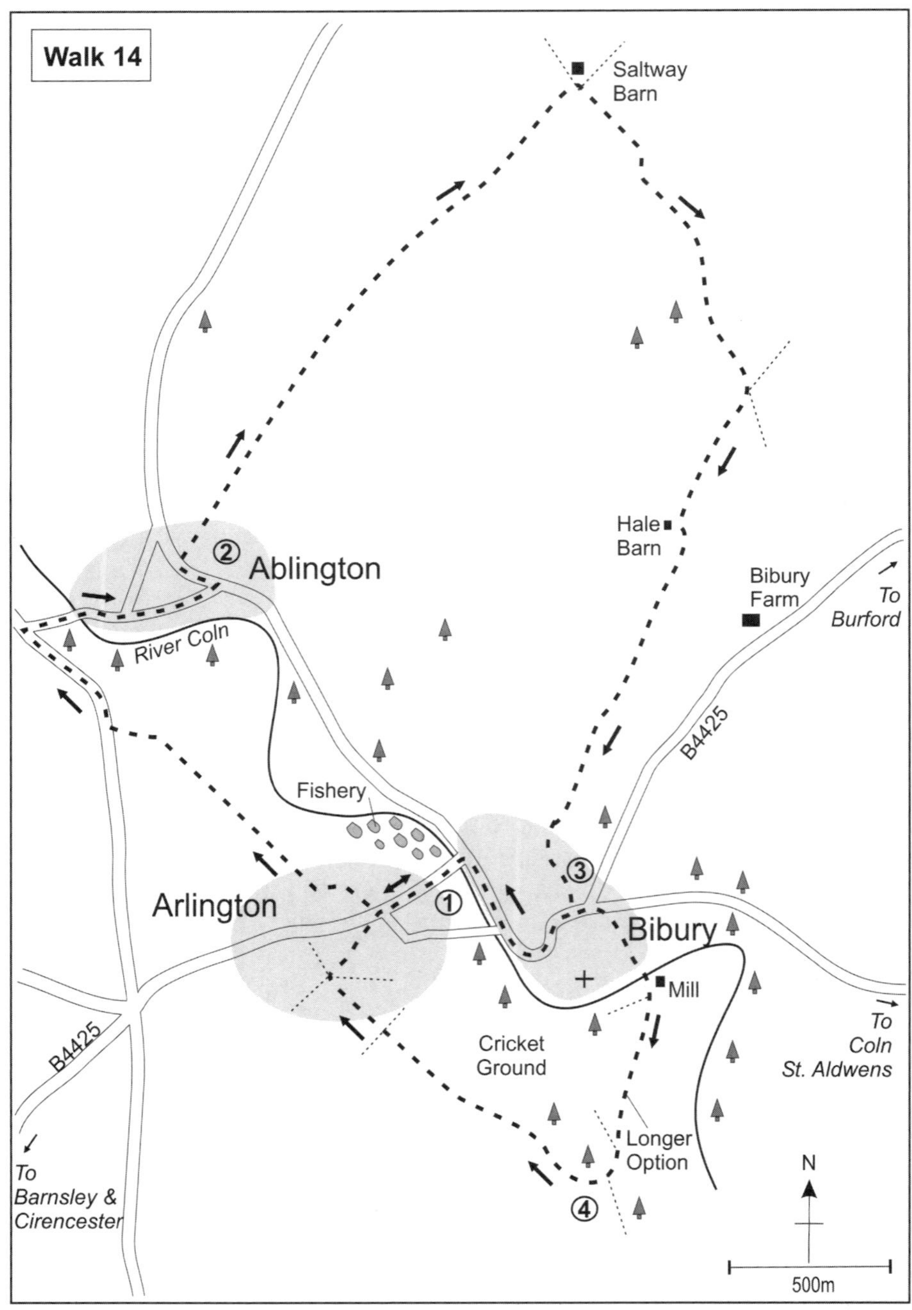
Walk 14
Saltway Barn
Hale Barn
Ablington
Bibury Farm
To Burford
River Coln
B4425
Fishery
Arlington
Bibury
Mill
Cricket Ground
To Coln St. Aldwens
B4425
To Barnsley & Cirencester
Longer Option
N
500m

Barn, and then follow the track and keep straight ahead along the driveway and a track leading down into the village. Reach the first houses as we descend Packhorse Lane to Bibury, passing the Old Vicarage, an old manor house from about 1590, and also the Pigeon House behind the Old Vicarage. Go on down to the main road - and here is a point of decision.

Either turn right for the shorter option, or left if wishing to walk an extra 2.5 miles.

3. **If selecting the shorter option**, turn right to walk on the road and then alongside the river with Rack Island across to the left, and a Souvenir Shop on the right. You will see the friendly ducks, the very clear water in the river, and the good views across to Arlington Row.

   For the longer walk, turn left and after a few yards when the road divides, take the right fork signed to Coln St Aldwyns, Quenington and Hatherop - and after a few more yards turn right along the track - a Public Bridleway. This leads to the Mill, and over to the right can be seen Bibury Court. Cross the river, pass the mill and follow the track as it climbs up away from the river. At the top a footpath forks right but we keep straight ahead, along the broad track. Across the field to the left is the Coln and the steep wooded bluff on the far bank. The track divides and we keep straight ahead, with a sheep fold on our right. The track begins to climb, with trees on both sides - and a very good view back to where we have walked from. Near the top of the woods the track divides and we take the right fork.

4. As we bend round to the right, emerge from the wood, with an open field on our left. Pass through a gate, with a low wall on our right, and a wood beyond the wall - colourful with bluebells in spring. Pass a gate on our right, with views across to the cricket pitch and the pavilion, but keep straight ahead. Go over a stone slab stile by a metal gate and continue alongside the wall. Pass the end of the wood, still with the wall, and keep straight ahead as we approach the houses and the road. Turn right here and walk back to the starting point, passing the narrow road to our left which was our route at the beginning of the walk - with the Old Post Office on the corner. Then we reach the Catherine Wheel on our right. Just beyond here is the narrow road and at this point either go straight on to complete the walk, or detour to

walk past Arlington Row. For this detour, climb up past a converted barn, to Awkward Hill. When the road bends left (on this bend is the footpath sign to Ready Token) start to descend to Arlington Row, and thence back to our starting point.

Arlington Row of cottages dating from 1380s

Not to be missed

Bibury church

To visit the church walk alongside the main road and the river, with Arlington Row on the right. Pass the village hall, with its tidy garden, and reach Church Barn and the Primary School adjacent to the church of St Mary the Virgin. Just beyond the church is Bibury Court, which dates from Tudor time, the main building being by Sir Thomas Sackville in 1633. The church of St Mary has Saxon origins, and outside the church can be seen a Saxon gravestone in the north wall of the chancel. Fragments of other gravestones can be seen just inside the south door, but these are only casts, as the originals are in the British Museum. Amongst the gravestones in the churchyard are some large table tombs, some with barrel tops and others with the bale tops, thought to have been evidence of the burial of a rich wool merchant, but probably simply as a form of decoration. Inside the church are many features of interest, dating back through the centuries. The chancel arch has square Saxon jambs and imposts and the 13th century saw a new chancel arch on the Saxon work. There is Norman work in the nave, and the unusual square font is from the 13th century. The lancet windows in the chancel date from that time too, and the one to the north side has a Parsons stained glass window dating from 1927, and part of this was used on the Christmas stamps of 1992. The Perpendicular style windows in the South Aisle date from the 15th century.

The Trout Farm

Open daily though with shorter hours in the winter. Phone 01285 740215. One of Britain's oldest Trout Farms – founded in 1902 to help stock local rivers with brown trout. Now covers 15 acres and has café, play area, shop, home made ice cream, sells fish and gives an opportunity to feed the fish (and the ducks which nip in for food) - and even catch a fish. The hatchery spawns up to six million trout ova every year.

Walk 15
Fairford and the Cotswold Water Park

From the beautiful stone Cotswold market town we take a gentle walk along the Coln, into part of the Cotswold Water Park and circle back into Fairford.

Starting point	**The signed free car park just beyond the church and close to the entrance to Fairford Park. Grid reference 152013. This environmentally friendly car park has grass growing between the small concrete blocks**
Maps	**OS Landranger 163; Explorer OL45**
How to get there	**Along the A417 between Cirencester and Lechlade**
Distance	**Just over 4 miles**
Time	**2 hours of easy walking**
Terrain	**Very gentle with no hills, but may be muddy**
Refreshments	**Fairford – a choice of pubs and cafés**
Nearest TIC	**Cirencester (01285 654180)**

The small market town of Fairford is tucked away in the heart of the Cotswolds and deep in the south east corner of Gloucestershire. One of many attractive settlements in the Cotswolds, Fairford is situated on the River Coln, just above its confluence with the Thames, and close to several lakes of the Fairford-Lechlade Eastern section of the Cotswold Water Park. A town of oolitic limestone buildings, some of which date from the 17th and 18th centuries, Fairford is a very clean and tidy town with many delightful buildings. Outstanding is the restored Mill on the Coln at the fringe of the town on the edge of Fairford Park. Here, birds and fish can be seen in the mill pond - the large trout possibly having arrived as escapees from the fish farm upstream at Bibury. Even more impressive is

St Mary's church, which dates from the 15th century and was built to replace an earlier structure.

The walk

1. Start from the car park, facing the magnificent church, and turn right along the road to walk to the restored Mill House. On the right here is Fairford Park, now managed by the Ernest Cook Trust. Ernest Cook bought the Estate in 1945, and later put it into the trust which has taken his name. It is a charity which supports various educational projects. We cross over the River Coln as we walk on for 100 yards beyond the mill pond, and reach the small picnic area at the Oxpens, ancient stalls formerly used by cattle. Opposite these we turn left, over a stone stile into the large meadow - still part of the Ernest Cook Trust land. At the end of this field is a remarkable hanging chain stile, which is easily pulled open. After a few yards of narrow path and then a stone stile we reach the main road. Cross straight over and continue along the narrow road - Waterloo Lane. The road soon ends and we walk

Restored Oxpens

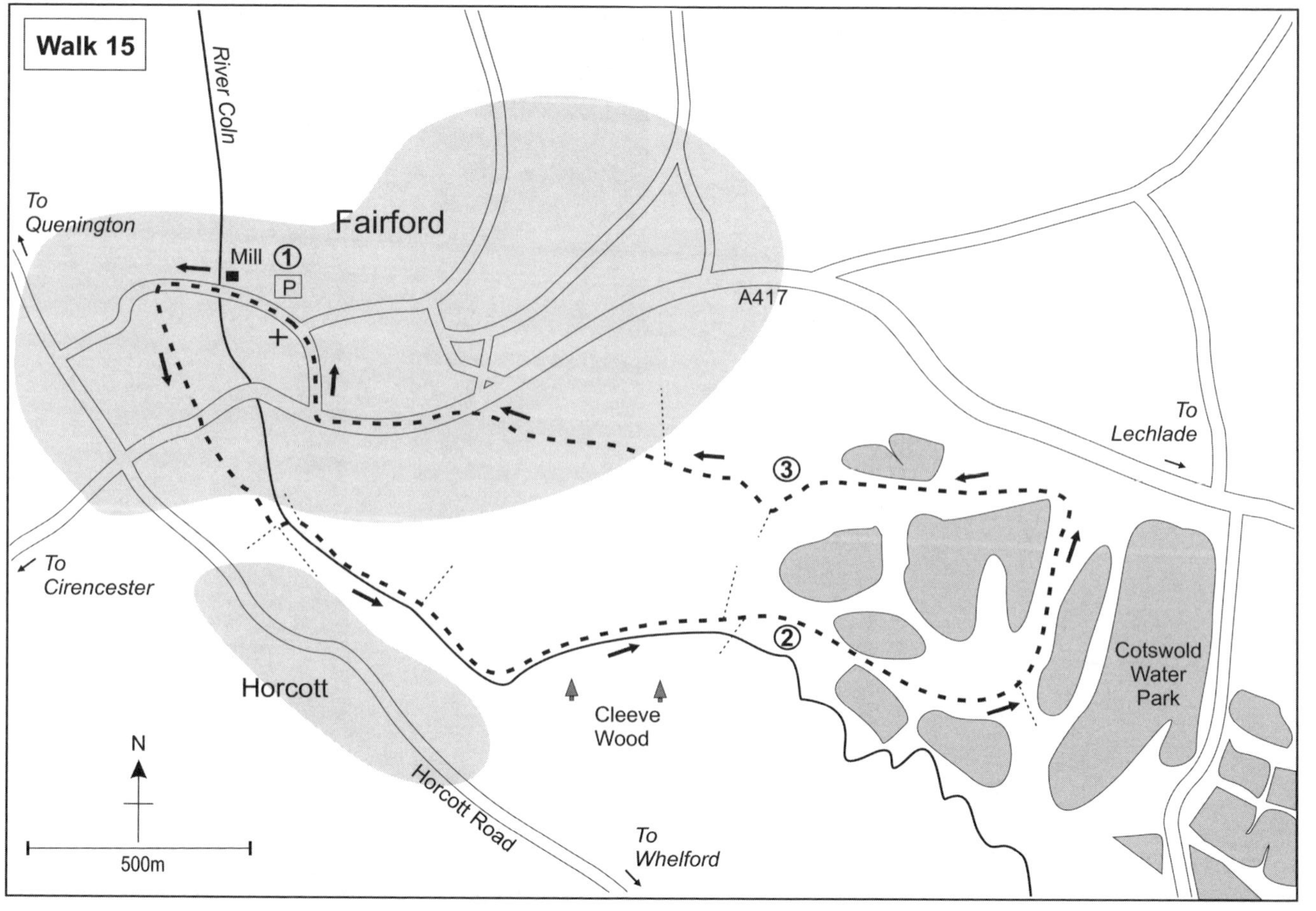
Walk 15
River Coln
To Quenington
Fairford
Mill
P
A417
To Lechlade
To Cirencester
Horcott
Cleeve Wood
Cotswold Water Park
N
500m
Horcott Road
To Whelford

along a narrow footpath, with playing fields on the right and then a small garden on the left, part of the local school river bank project. Turn left over the metal footbridge - Dilly's Bridge - and cross both channels of the river, then turn right to walk alongside the river, now on our right. Pass a long garden on our left and then the delightful house on the opposite bank, as we walk on to emerge from the trees, into open meadow land - still close to the river bank. Keep ahead along the bank, on the edge of a grassy meadow. The attractive and fast flowing stream is very clear, and home for many insects and fish, and the bank is lined with trees and bushes ideal for a variety of birds. Look into the clear water of the river as there are likely to be trout lurking - and unseen - until you look very carefully.

2. Follow the riverside path until reaching a small footbridge going left (a few yards before reaching a larger footbridge) and we turn left here, towards a large lake. This is lake number 104, one of the more than 140 lakes in the Cotswold Water Park - a larger water area than in the

View of lakein the Cotswold Water Park

Norfolk Broads and catering for all sorts of leisure activities. A few yards beyond the bridge the path divides and we turn right. Follow the fenced footpath with the lake about 30 yards to the left. The lake is home to a wide range of waterfowl. The path leads us round the lake margin and another lake can soon be seen to the right. Our path is lined with bushes and undergrowth, a nature paradise, and is loud with the sounds of birds in spring and summer, including many summer visiting warblers.

To the right is a smaller narrow lake (103), used for fishing, and beyond that, further to the right is lake 105 used by water skiers. Lake 104 is quiet, except for the noise of the birds. The path bends round to the left and after turning slightly right the path divides and we take the left fork, still following the shore of the lake. As we bend further to the left, noise of the main road (A417) can be heard over to our right. We are now on the far side of the lake from where we were a few minutes ago, but just continue along the fenced path, with open meadows on our right.

3. The path continues between a fence and a hedge, with a small lake just visible on our right. Walk through a few trees and emerge to an open field and a T-junction in the path. Turn right here along the field margin and after a few yards pass through a gate and follow the path which bends left between two open fields. On our right is the town football pitch with its tall poles for floodlighting. At the end of the pitch a clear track goes off to the right, but we keep straight ahead along a tree-lined broad path. At a junction of paths keep straight ahead through a wooden kissing gate and along the margin of a small field to another kissing gate and the first houses of Fairford. Continue between houses and turn right at a slightly major road and then bend left to reach the main road. The Eight Bells is on our right (phone 01285 712369). Turn left along the main road to walk back into the centre of the town between stone houses and colourful gardens, passing the Library and Police Station – and Palmer Hall, which was provided by Colonel Palmer of the Huntley and Palmer biscuit company in 1936. Pass, or visit, the Plough Inn, another of the excellent pubs in Fairford (phone 01285 712409), and turn right at the Market Place On the left is the Bull Hotel (phone 01285 712535) and next is the 18th century building of Fairford Free School, now a Heritage and Community Centre, before reaching the church – which MUST be visited.

Not to be missed

St Mary's church with its prominent pinnacled tower is most famous for its complete set of medieval stained glass windows – the only complete set in a Parish church in Britain. St Mary's was rebuilt by John Tame, a local wool merchant, in the 1490s and the glass was installed in the 15 years after rededication in 1497. Much of the glass has been beautifully restored by Keith Barley, over a 20 year period. In addition to the glass the church has a fine collection of misericords and other wooden and stone work, including the Lygon Tomb in the Lady Chapel, and a memorial to John Keble, who was born in Fairford in 1792. He was one of the founders of the Oxford Movement and has an Oxford college named after him. Just outside the porch is a small stone memorial to the church cat and from here can be seen several of the carvings (some grotesque) on the tower.

Stone memorial to the Church cat

Kelmscott

Kelmscott Manor was the home of William Morris, and he, his wife Jane, children Jenny and May are buried at St George's Church in the village. The house was built of local stone about 1600, with later additions, and has beautiful gardens, a dovecote and is close to the River Thames. The main building is a Grade I listed farmhouse. It is open to the public but with restricted opening times – April to September every Wednesday and 1st and 3rd Saturdays in each month (phone 01367 252486). In the time of William Morris the house was a centre for talented artists and designers, notably Dante Gabriel Rossetti and Burne-Jones. Wonderful examples of their furniture, pictures, textiles, metalwork etc. can be seen on a tour of the house. The village of Kelmscott contains cottages designed by Webb and Gimson who were much involved in the Arts and Crafts movement which was so strong in the Cotswolds.

Walk 16
Sapperton

From the delightful stone village of Sapperton hidden in a narrow valley, we descend steeply to walk along the route of the old Severn-Thames canal, before climbing back out of the valley to cross parkland of the Bathurst Estate.

Starting point	Grid reference 948034, close to the church
Maps	OS Explorer 168; Landranger 163
How to get there	From the A417 north west of Cirencester follow signs to Daglingworth, ignoring the turn off the island signed to Daglingworth Village and taking the next turn off the island which is signed to Daglingworth, beyond which follow the signs to Sapperton along narrow roads. Alternative approach from Cirencester by taking the A419 towards Chalford and after 4 miles fork right for Sapperton
Distance	4.5 miles
Time	2 hours
Terrain	Steep descent to the canal and then a climb back up to the open ground. Clear paths, but can be muddy
Refreshments	Pub at Daneway on the walk (01285 760297) or the pub in Sapperton (The Bell 01285 760298). Alternative starting place using The Bell car park - with permission
Nearest TICs	Cirencester (01285 654180) and Stroud (01453 760900)

Sapperton

The stone houses in this traditional Cotswold village date from 17th century and later, though many have been changed over the years. Sapperton became a centre for the Cotswold Arts and Crafts movement at the end of the 19th century and into the 20th century. The leader was Ernest Gimson (1864-1919) who lived at the old Elizabethan Pinbury House (also the home of John Masefield for a time) in Pinbury Park, on the edge of the Bathurst Estate, from 1894-1901. By 1900 the craft community was growing, under the patronage of Lord Bathurst, and the lack of space at Pinbury resulted in the move to Sapperton. Daneway House, which dated from the 13th or 14th century, was lent to the group by Lord Bathurst and it became the workshop and showrooms for their designs. Ernest and Sidney Barnsley as well as Norman Jewson moved to houses in Sapperton where many buildings were designed or partially designed by these craftsmen. Upper Dorvel house, built in 1903 and occupied by Ernest Barnsley, consisted of two original cottages with additions at each end. Other buildings where they worked include Beechanger (Sidney Barnsley worked on it and lived in it), The Leasowes, a Cottage on the Green (Ernest Barnsley), the Village Hall (Ernest Barnsley). Bachelors Court was altered by Norman Jewson (1884-1975). The Sapperton workshops closed when Gimson died (at Daneway House in 1919), but many of the craftsmen went to Chalford, with Peter van deer Waal, who had been Gimson's chief cabinet maker.

The walk

1. Park by the church of St Kenelm. With the church on the right, walk from the telephone box and road junction, straight ahead and after about 20 yards a Public Footpath sign points right and we turn here. Go down quite steeply between attractive stone houses - cross a narrow road and keep ahead on the narrow path between fences. The path becomes very stony and quite uneven until we reach a kissing gate, beyond which is an open field. Walk diagonally across the field, descending towards the woods. Go on over the stile into the woods and walk over the top of the tunnel. The path bends right and leads alongside the route of the old canal and we can see the opening into the tunnel. This became blocked by rock falls but was formerly the route of the canal, through which the boats were powered by the leggers. With a length of 2 miles 288 yards, it was dug by hand, and completed in 1789. The other end of the tunnel is close to the source

of the Thames. Used from 1789 till 1911, the boats were propelled by bargees lying on their backs and using their legs on the roof to provide propulsion. Over the entrance to the tunnel is a small plaque. The Daneway Portal to the Sapperton Tunnel was restored by the Cotswold Canal Trust and unveiled by Lord Apsley on 21st September, 1996. The tunnel provided the link between the Stroudwater Canal (opened in 1779) and the Thames, which completed the Severn-Thames water link. The canal closed in 1927, though some small stretches have been restored. The growth of railways removed the need for the canals.

The view down to the canal

Continue along a fairly level clear path through the trees, with a small stream on our left and the old canal on our right. Trees and undergrowth provide a haven for wildlife – with wild flowers and singing birds making this ideal for spring and early summer walking. Reach a stile, where we see the sign for Gloucestershire Wildlife Trust Nature Reserve, and come out of trees into an open field, and arrive at a large white building, the Daneway Inn, close to one of the 40 locks

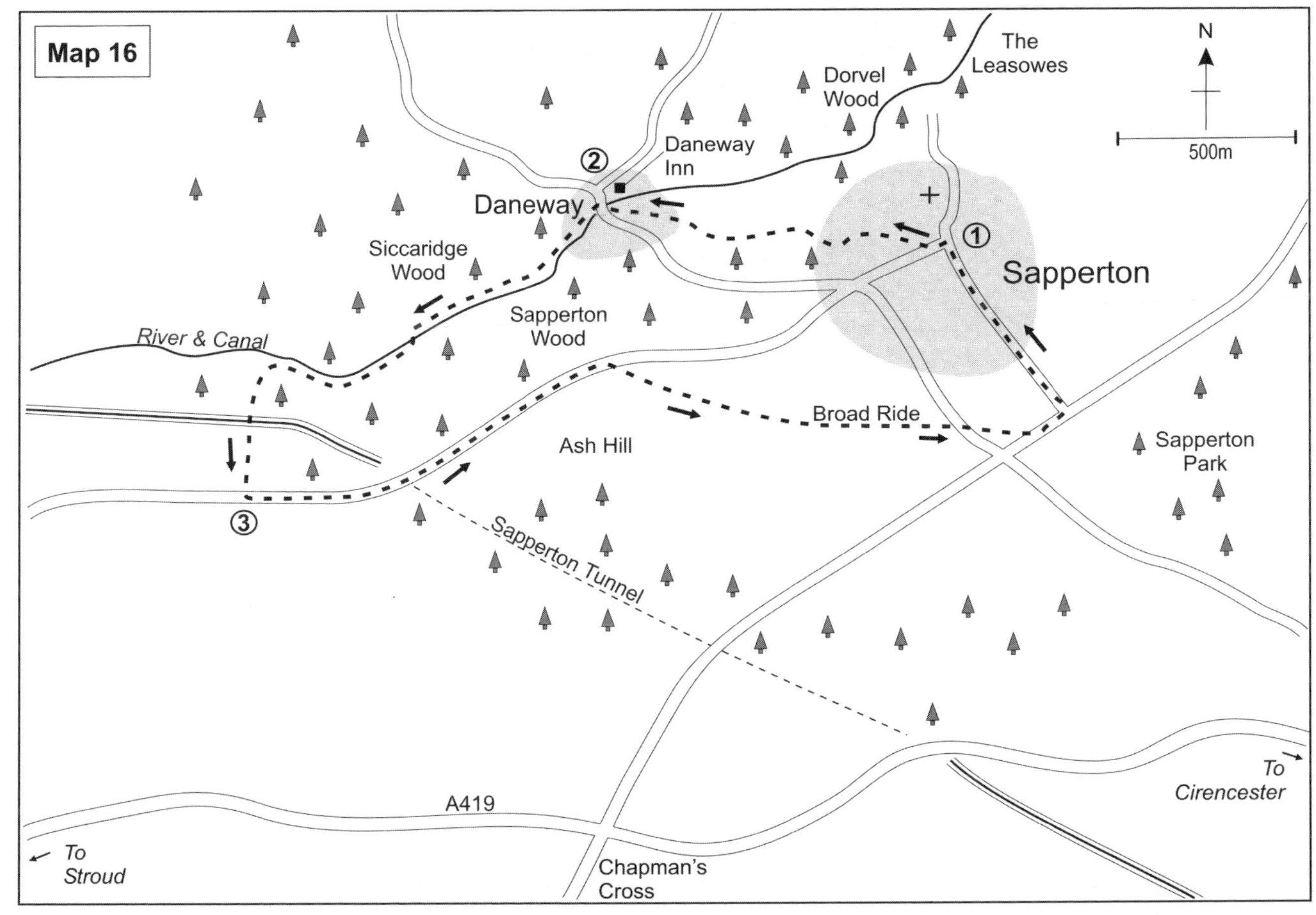

Map 16
The Leasowes
Dorvel Wood
N
500m
②
Daneway Inn
Daneway
①
Sapperton
Siccaridge Wood
Sapperton Wood
River & Canal
Broad Ride
Ash Hill
Sapperton Park
③
Sapperton Tunnel
To Cirencester
A419
To Stroud
Chapman's Cross

which raised the canal up to the height of the tunnel. Formerly three small cottages this was turned into a pub, very popular with the bargees and leggers who took the barges through the tunnel. On the hill behind the pub is the SSSI Of Daneway Banks noted for its limestone grassland and associated plants as well as yellow meadow ants. The magnificent old Daneway House is close too.

2. The path leads to the road bridge where we cross the road, turn right for a few yards, and then left, to continue along the right side of the canal, between a small wall and fence. A warning notice mentions the dangers of the old locks, which are very deep. Another Nature Reserve sign emphasises that this is an outstanding area for wild life - and we soon reach a large information board about Siccarage Wood and Sapperton Valley. The valley contain numerous swamps and pools, and Siccarage Wood is a limestone coppiced woodland, with several outstanding plants notably Lilies of the Valley - best seen in May. Rock was quarried from Siccarage for building the tunnel. Pass a few old locks which create their own microclimate with lush growth of mosses in the dark and damp location. Continue through the woods, until we reach a footbridge where our path turns left, and then right, on the other side of canal - really keeping straight ahead. On the footbridge is the logo sign of Wysis Way, a long distance footpath which links Offa's Dyke to the Thames Path. Reach an information board, and a bridge over the canal where several paths meet - and we turn left. After about 20 yards at a T-junction where clear tracks go left and right, we go straight ahead over a stile and into the Bathurst Estate, along the narrow path which is beginning to climb. This is a fairly steep climb through the trees, and to our left is a small stream which has cut a valley. The climb takes us up to the busy Cheltenham to Swindon railway line, which we cross, over two strong metal stiles. Notice to our left, the opening of a tunnel. The climb continues, using a few wooden steps in places, to reach a narrow road where we turn left.

3. As we walk along this we can enjoy the more open views across the surrounding countryside. After about half a mile along this road, where it bends to the right, on the right is a parking area and Public Bridleway sign. We fork right here to walk along the Broad Ride, a grassy avenue flanked by trees. Stay on this straight grassy and level stretch for half a mile, to reach a road - and cross over to continue straight ahead to reach another road. The Broad Ride continues beyond here, straight

View along the broad ride

ahead into Oakley Wood and Cirencester Park but we turn left along the road. After about 100 yards turn left again towards Sapperton, and walk 300 yards into the village, passing The Bell on the way.

Not to be missed

St Kenelm's church is one of very few churches with this name, and the shrine of this boy king of Mercia was in Winchcombe Abbey. A few pieces of stonework date from Norman times, but the church was mostly rebuilt in the 14th century, with further changes made by the Atkyns family in the early 18th century. The shape is asymmetric cruciform with a central tower and a broach spire. North and South transepts contain memorials, to the Poole family in the north transept and Sir Robert Atkyns in the south. Atkyns lived in the Sapperton Manor House which was acquired by the first Lord Bathurst in 1730s, soon after which it was demolished. Lord Bathurst gave much of the carved wood to the church, some of which can

Memorial

be seen in the Bathurst pew up on the Gallery and the bench ends of the pews with their Jacobean figures.

In the churchyard notice the base and shaft of 15th century cross, and look at the fine collection of brass memorial plates. Just inside the churchyard beneath the yew trees are the tombs of both Barnsleys on one side and Gimson on the other side of the path, with very plain gravestones. There are many more memorial plates which are difficult to read but date back to the late 17th century. Beneath the other yew trees closer to the door of the church are more memorials including two very fossiliferous stones, and several memorials to the Stratfords from 1771. There are several to the Kimbers and the Yarnton family, who also have a memorial inside the church.

Corinium Museum in Cirencester

Several features of interest in Cirencester but top of the list is the remarkable Museum, refurbished in 2002-2004. Several earlier museums were incorporated into this modern museum which contains displays of various periods in the local history. The original museums were created by the two private collections of the Bathurst family and then the Cripps. Outstanding of all the displays in the museum are the Roman remains, as Cirencester was the second largest town in that period of history.

Walk 17
Woodchester

The walk takes us round the Woodchester Estate in a secluded valley south of Stroud and west of Nailsworth. We walk through the deciduous woodlands on the valley side and along the valley floor close to the man-made lakes, and pass Woodchester Mansion with its remarkable history.

Starting point	**The large car park for Woodchester Mansion: grid reference 799014 – £2 but free to National Trust members**
Maps	**OS Landranger 162; Explorer 168**
How to get there	**Leave the M5 aT-junction 13 and take the A417 towards Stroud. Turn right signed to Eastington at the first traffic island, then follow signs to Frocester. Keep straight ahead through Frocester and climb steeply up the Cotswold scarp. Reach a T-junction at the top and turn left along the B4066. After about 400 yards where the Coaley Peak viewpoint is on the left, turn right signed to Woodchester Park**
Distance	**5 miles**
Time	**2-3 hours**
Terrain	**Dry and firm paths, even in wet spells of weather. Also, as it is mainly in woods, is sheltered from cold and windy weather – but is at its most magnificent in dry weather**
Refreshments	**Rose and Crown pub in Nympsfield (phone 01453 860240): snacks available in the Mansion on open days**
Nearest TIC	**Stroud (phone 01453 760960)**

Woodchester Park was bought by the National Trust in 1994 with the aim of preserving the old and special landscape. The Park is open every day, but the Mansion, not National Trust, is only open on specified days (phone 01453 861541). From the mid 17th until mid 19th centuries the Park was owned by the Ducie family, who built a house and created a landscaped park with formal gardens, fishponds and carriage drives through the surrounding woodlands. The estate was bought by William Leigh, a wealthy ship owner from Liverpool, in 1845. He demolished the house and was building a Victorian Gothic Mansion in its place, with Benjamin Bucknall as the architect. This was never finished as he abandoned the project after 16 years work, leaving the unfinished building deserted.

Leigh chose to live in Park House, later known as The Cottage, at the top of the valley above the Mansion. Meanwhile the abandoned incomplete house began to decay, until the Woodchester Mansion Trust was founded to protect and preserve the building.

The varied wildlife in the Park includes buzzards, owls and woodpeckers in the woods and ducks and other water birds on the lakes. Summer visiting birds are numerous, as are badgers, but most famous of all are the bats, which live in the house.

The walk

1. At the car park is an Information Board, with a map. Go down the steps to the main drive - turn right and walk downhill through the beautiful deciduous woodland, where there are masses of wild flowers in spring and also noisy bird song. When the track divides take the left fork following the blue route as marked on the post and begin to walk uphill - still in the woods. On the left pass the small Marmontsflat quarry which was a source of stone for the estate buildings. Then reach a seat and a viewpoint looking right across the valley. Continue along the drive and then bend right and descend, still following the blue arrow. At a T-junction the blue turns right but we go left following orange and red. The old ice house was situated down to our right, but there is nothing to see from our path. The path becomes fairly level as it bends right round the top of a valley, and we just follow the arrows passing a few redwood trees on our right. The track bends round to the right and heads down to the valley. At the main track the house is visible to our right, but we turn left. Walk along the valley and pass the first lake to our right - Brick Kiln Pond, the first of the series of five man-made lakes. Pass some steps heading down to our right - the path we shall

be following later on our return walk. The second lake - Old Pond - is down to the right and on the left is Break Heart Hill, and on a post can be seen the small sign of a butterfly. In the cleared south facing area wild flowers grow well and attract many butterflies on the sunny days of spring and early summer. Here and elsewhere on the walk are useful information notices. Follow the track as it bends round to the right where the red route is signed to the left - but we still follow the orange route. The track soon divides and orange goes right and heads down to the lake, but we go left along the red route to pass an ancient stone seat (restored in 2003) with good views across to the right. Look for the arms of the Nympsfield windmill, built in 1996, which might just be visible above the trees at the top of the valley opposite.

2. We continue straight ahead and then bend round to the right to reach a junction of tracks where a track does go straight ahead but we turn sharp right to start on our return journey. Soon emerge from the

Looking down at one of the lakes

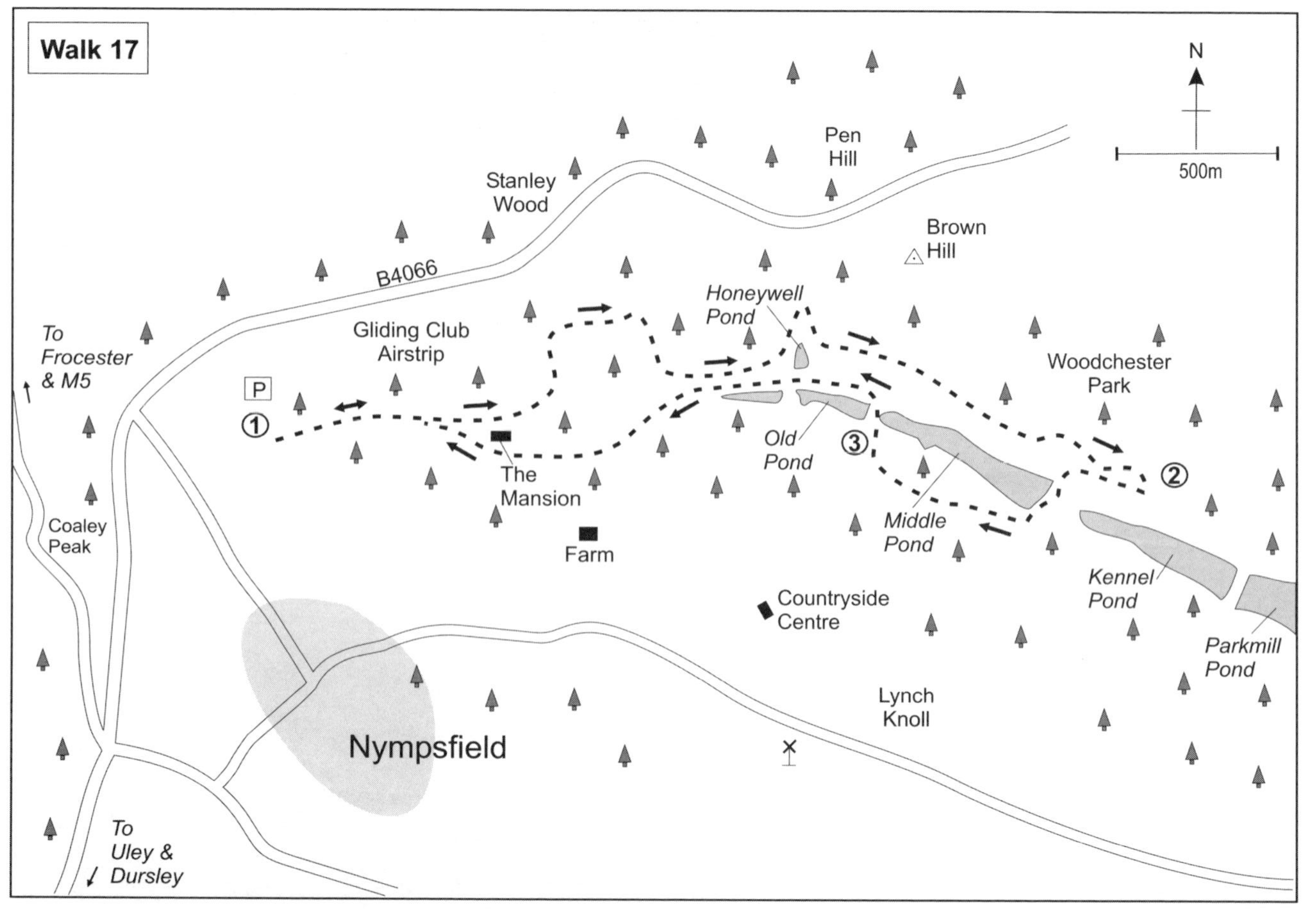

Walk 17
N
500m
Pen Hill
Stanley Wood
Brown Hill
B4066
Honeywell Pond
Gliding Club Airstrip
To Frocester & M5
Woodchester Park
P
1
3
2
Old Pond
The Mansion
Coaley Peak
Middle Pond
Farm
Kennel Pond
Countryside Centre
Parkmill Pond
Lynch Knoll
Nympsfield
To Uley & Dursley

woods to reach an open area where the large dam is on our left. Turn left here to cross the dam with good views right along the length of Middle Pond (the third of the five lakes), with the Boat House at the far end. Trees on our left prevent us from getting a sight of the Kennel Lake, but we carry on across the dam and turn right through a large wooden gate to walk into the field. The path takes us across the middle of the field to a gate at the far end, and along a narrow path close to the lake. Climb up a few steps and turn right across the dam, with the 19th century, but recently restored, Old Boathouse just to our right, and views back down the lake – the Middle Pond. Bats roost in the roof space of the Boathouse. Birds which may be seen on the lakes include tufted duck, mallard, coot, moorhen, heron and possibly sightings of kingfisher or the summer visiting sandpiper.

3. Once across the dam turn left, by the paddle sign for the Boathouse, and follow the orange arrow. Old Pond is to our left as we walk on, through a gate and out of the woods, across an open meadow and then

The boat house

up the steps to the main track. Turn left here and follow the driveway to the house, possibly seeing cattle and sheep in the neighbouring meadows. In addition to helping to preserve the pastures the animals attract flies which provide food for the bats. Keep looking up in the sky to see if there are any gliders flying from the airfield which is just to the north of the Woodchester Estate close to the road leading to Stroud. Work is still continuing on the house but if it is open it is well worth a visit. Even just walking past, the grand design of the building can be admired, together with the unusual grotesque gargoyles, and monkeys on the pinnacles. But otherwise continue along the main drive for three quarters of a mile and climb steadily through the woods back to the car park

Not to be missed

Woodchester Mansion still looks magnificent from the outside, with glass in the ground floor windows but open to the elements above. Described as a Gothic masterpiece untouched by time, it is being maintained in the state at which it was left, when Mr Leigh abandoned his project, possibly because his interest in, and generosity to, the Roman Catholic church had overstretched his finances.

Over the years the Mansion has had various uses but was beginning to decay and in 1986 the Stroud Council bought the house aided by grants from English Heritage. The Woodchester Mansion Trust was formed in 1989 and, in 1992, signed a 99 year lease on the Mansion. Many repairs have taken place since that time in order to preserve the house, as much as possible in its original, unfinished, state. It has become a centre for classes in stonemasonry and other conservation techniques, as well as being open to the public on many days between Easter and October, with special events such as bat walks and varied children's activities. The building is nationally famous for its bats, and is home to four varieties, notably the rare Greater Horseshoe all of which are now ringed as part of an ongoing study.

Woodchester mansion

The other varieties are the Lesser Horseshoe, the Pipistrelle and Brown Long-Eared Bats. There is a special Bat Observatory in the room next to the bathroom and a Batcam provides views of the bats for visitors to see.

Woodchester Village is not accessible from Woodchester Mansion but can be reached along the A46 two miles south of Stroud. The village is famous for its Roman villa which was situated in what is now the old churchyard in North Woodchester. The Romans were here from 2nd century AD, and the Villa contained the largest known Roman mosaic north of the Alps. It was first recorded in 1693 and excavated in 1712, but the main excavations came from Samuel Lysons from 1793-1797. The villa is not visible but some Roman bricks have been used in the old church and wall of culverts around the Old Priory Grounds.

To visit the site turn right off the main A46 along the narrow road into the village. Park on the right side just before reaching the village post office and shop, close to the sign pointing across the field to the Roman Villa. Cross the field to reach a narrow lane, turn right and there is the old church and the site of the villa. An information board gives a plan and a little of the history. The old church of St Mary was built on the site of an earlier chapel in the ruins of the Roman Villa, but by the mid 19th century was in a poor state of repair and only a few Norman fragments and other remains have survived, including the impressive table tombs. The new church was built closer to the main area of settlement by the architect S.S. Teulon in 1863-64, and contains many monuments from the old church. To visit the modern church retrace steps along the lane but do not cross the field. Pass stone houses and colourful gardens alongside Church Lane, and at the main street the spire of the new St Mary can be seen. Walk along Church Road past the village pub and village hall to visit the well cared for new church.

Walk 18
Wotton-under-Edge

The walk leads from the interesting town of Wotton up the steep slope of the Cotswold escarpment then across the plateau through woods and fields to reach the prominent Tyndale Memorial, before returning across the plateau and back down into the town – enjoying the wonderful views across the Severn valley to the hills of Wales.

Starting point	Grid reference 756932
Maps	OS Landranger 162 or 172; Explorer 167
How to get there	Leave the M6 at junction 14 and follow signs to Wotton-under-Edge, along B4509 at first and then the B4058. Follow signs in the town to the Chipping car park, in the old market place
Distance	5.5 miles
Time	2-3 hours
Terrain	Steep climb at the start, with the descent at the end of the walk, but mainly along the fairly level plateau surface. Clear paths but can become muddy in stretches through the woods
Refreshments	Good selection in Wotton
Nearest TIC	Stroud (01453 760960) and Nailsworth (01453 839222)

Wotton is not really in the Cotswolds, but sits at the foot of the edge, which is the scarp forming the western end of the hills. The ancient settlement of Wotton was badly damaged by enemies of the Berkeleys but it was then rebuilt in 1253. There have been close links with the Berkeleys throughout the centuries. Thomas Lord Berkeley (1352-1417) is buried in the church, and a school was created by Katherine Lady Berkeley in 1384.

The present day school still takes her name. Amongst the interesting old buildings in the town are the 17th century Manor House which was lived in by the Berkeleys. The Old Court, Bluecoat School and Tolsey House will be passed on the walk but a gentle perambulation round the town will reveal many other interesting buildings including the Alms Houses on Church Street, a gift from Hugh Perry in 1638 and extended by Thomas Dawes in the 18th century.

The Walk

1. Starting from the Chipping car park (free at time of last walk), walk past the Heritage Centre where there is a town and street map on the wall. Pass the Cinema and Star Inn on Market Street, and in the distance can be seen the church which we shall pass near the end of the walk. At the T-junction, turn left beneath the large Victorian Jubilee clock. Walk up to a major road signed to Dursley, but cross straight over and walk along Bradley Street and follow the sign for the Cotswold Way. Climbing slightly we reach a junction of roads and fork slightly right to climb up to the main road – Gloucester Street. Turn left here and soon pass the Old London Road and a few yards beyond here our path turns off to the right – following the Cotswold way sign pointing to North Nibley 2 miles. Climb very steeply along a narrow enclosed path, with a handrail. Go on through a small wooden gate and continue climbing. Cross over a narrow lane and keep ahead up steps, through another gate and follow the steep path through the trees to the top of Wotton Hill. Emerge on to a grassy patch with a circular walled enclosure a few yards to our left. This is the Jubilee Clump. The information board tells us that trees were planted here in 1815 to commemorate the victory at Waterloo. They had become thinner by the end of the Crimea War and were felled for a bonfire. More trees were planted to commemorate the Jubilee of Queen Victoria in 1887. Enjoy the wonderful views from here across the Severn Plain.

Cotswold way sign at start of the walk

Jubilee Clump

2. Continue up to the top right corner of the grassy patch to reach a wooden kissing gate and the sign for the Cotswold Way (yellow arrow with white dot on it) which we continue to follow. We are now on the plateau and walk along the left side of a large cropped field, with woods and steep slope to our left. Our return route will take us along the far side of this field. Reach a junction of paths at the end of the field, where we keep straight ahead on the broad path overhung with branches – and still an open field to our right. As we reach the end of this field the broad path divides and we take the left fork to pass the site of Brackenbury Ditches, an ancient Iron Age Camp. Now a Scheduled Ancient Monument this was one of the line of hill forts situated along the top edge of the Cotswold scarp, looking out across to the Severn. The fort covers about eight acres surrounded by ramparts and ditches. The entrance is at the southern end.

The path divides as we reach the fort and we take the right fork, still on the Cotswold Way, with a large embankment on our left. As this embankment bends away to our left, we reach a junction of four

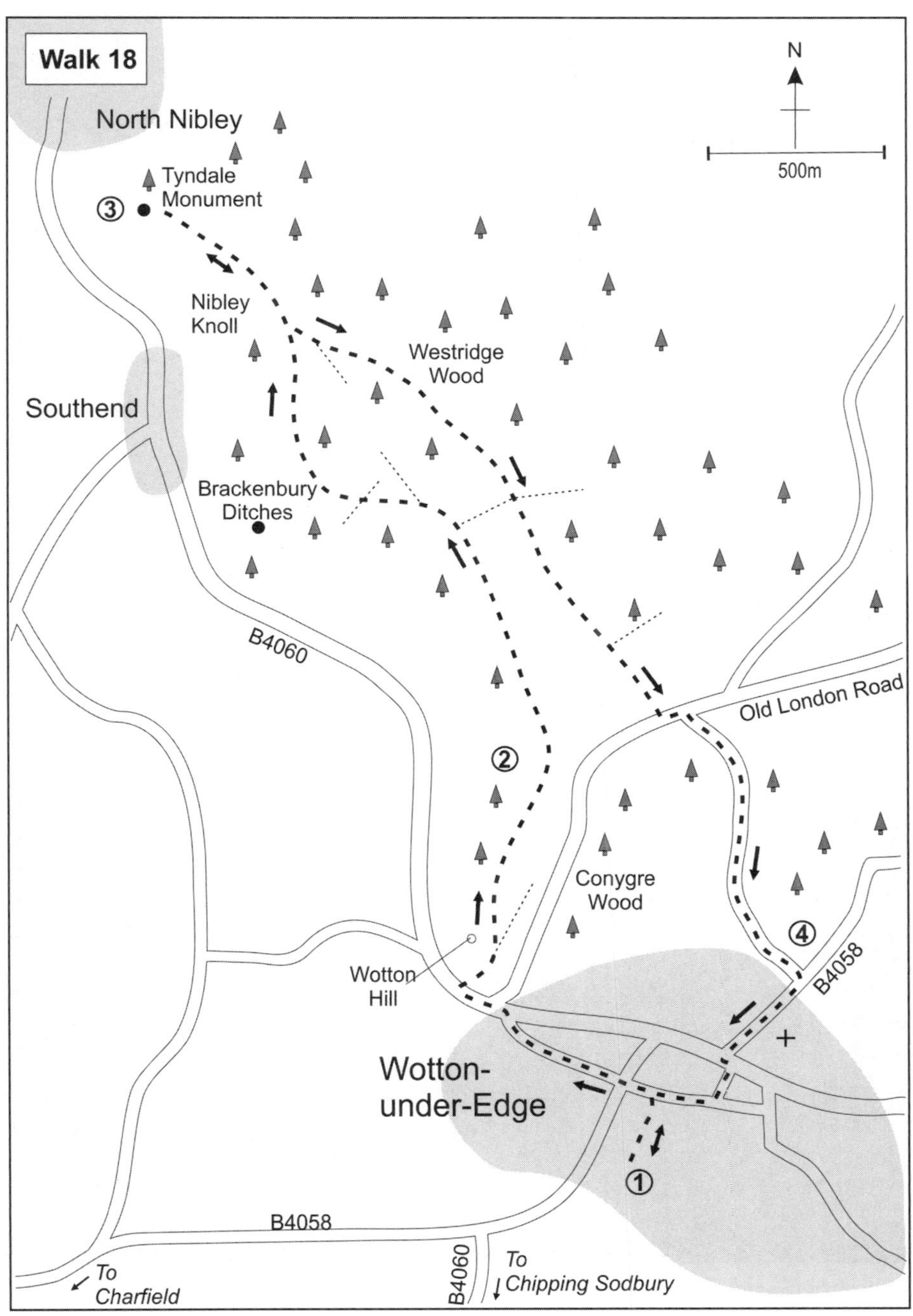
Walk 18
N
500m
North Nibley
Tyndale
Monument
③
Nibley
Knoll
Westridge
Wood
Southend
Brackenbury
Ditches
B4060
Old London Road
②
Conygre
Wood
④
B4058
Wotton
Hill
Wotton-
under-Edge
①
B4058
B4060
To
Charfield
To
Chipping Sodbury

Tynedale memorial

paths and just keep straight ahead. Soon bend slightly left to emerge from the woods on to an open grassy patch – and there is the Tyndale monument. A toposcope points out many of the features to be seen, including the Severn Bridge, Oldbury Power Station and Sugarloaf Hill, 33 miles away near Abergavenny. The Cotswold Way continues northwards but we turn back here, after enjoying the views and perhaps climbing to the top of the tower if it is open, for even better views.

William Tyndale was born in about 1484, possibly in North Nibley. His ambition was to translate the *Bible* into English so that everyone could read it. This monument in his memory was built in the 19th century, the foundation stone being laid on 29th May, 1863 by the Hon. Colonel Berkeley. He died, as a martyr, at Vilvoorden near Brussels in Belgium, in October 1536. The Tyndale Memorial is a 111 foot high tower, built of Cotswold stone, with an Italianate upper part with arrow slit windows and a Gothic Victorian lower part.

Above the doorway is a carving which tells us that Tyndale was the first translator of the *English Bible*. It was his life's work, and he wished to make it possible for 'the New Testament to be printed in the Mother Tongue of this country'. This was seen as a crime and he was burnt at the stake.

3. Retrace steps away from the monument and in addition to the wonderful views to the right over the plain, and the continuation of the Cotswold scarp extending away to the south towards Chipping Sodbury, views open up to the west and the BT mast near Newark and Ozleworth. We reach the end of the grassy summit area and enter the woods where we walked earlier. At a junction of paths, where the Cotswold Way forks right heading in a southerly direction, we take the left fork, heading south east through the Westridge Woods, which are rich in flowers and bird life. After about 30 yards this path divides and we take the left fork, and at the next junction take the right fork. This leads to a cross paths where we keep straight ahead along a broad track, floored by stones, remnants of an old track. Still heading in a south easterly direction we reach the edge of the woods, and walk along the left side of a large open field, which we saw earlier as we walked along the opposite side of this field on our way to the Tyndale tower. Walk on through a large gate, and the track leads us to a narrow road where we turn left for 10 yards and then right to begin to go

downhill along this narrow road, Adeys Lane. We can soon see down to the valley on our right, and the rooftops of Wotton come into sight. Just after the steepest part of the descent a kissing gate on the right leads to a good viewing point with seats for resting if required. Back on the road we complete the descent to the town, passing the large Under the Hill House on the right and then forking right along a tarmac path towards the church, with the delightful old Alms houses, founded by Miss Ann Bearpacker in 1837.

4. Cross the road to the church and enter the churchyard. Beneath the first yew tree is a very unusual carved sculptured headstone, as well as many other headstones in this well cared for churchyard. The church of St Mary the Virgin dates from the 13th century, and the prominent tower dates from the 15th century. The large nave creates the feeling of space inside the church, with tall pillars reaching up to carvings including some grotesque ceiling bosses. A large tomb in the north east corner contains the tombs of Lord Thomas 'The Magnificent' Berkeley and his wife Margaret Delisle (1360-1392). Some of the decoration inside the church is the work of the Gimsons's Cotswold School of Craftsmen.

   Leave the church and turn left along the road towards the town centre. Opposite the church is the old Blue Coat School. Pass to the left of the War Memorial and keep straight ahead along Church Street. Pass the Falcon Inn on the left, and then turn right on Long Street, an important shopping street. Turn left along Market Street, just before reaching the big clock. Along here we pass or call in at the Swan (01453 843004), a former 17th century coaching inn, just a few yards before arriving back at the Chipping.

Not to be missed

Ozleworth and Newark

Leave Wotton-under-Edge on the B4058 heading north eastwards. After about three miles reach the A4135 at a crossroads, and turn right along the narrow road signed to Ozleworth and Newark Park. This leads to the GPO Tower which dates from 1965, and here the road divides. Left fork is to Ozleworth Park where the noted church of St Nicholas, built by Roger de Berkeley in the 12th century, earns a star in the Simon Jenkins book of England's 1000 Best Churches. Built by Roger de Berkeley in the 12th century, the oldest part of the church is the tall hexagonal tower (which is very rare) - with a chancel and nave added. The lower part of the tower may have been a fortified hunting lodge originally. The western arch leading to the nave is Early English, with zig-zag and chevron decoration. The south doorway is Norman - and there is a blocked up Norman doorway on the north side. The font is also Norman, from the early 13th century. The monuments include memorials to the Clutterbuck family of Newark. The churchyard is circular which may suggest it was the site of a Celtic religious building. Ozleworth Park gardens are occasionally open to the public (01453 845591).

Newark Park nearby is former hunting lodge set in rolling parkland. Now managed by the National Trust, but only open two or three days a week in summer (phone 01453 842644).

Walk 19
Somerford Keynes

A figure of eight walk around Somerton Keynes takes us past several of the lakes, alongside the infant Thames and through meadows and woodlands, all rich in flora and fauna.

Starting point	**At the Neigh Bridge Country Park close to the B4696. Grid reference 018947**
Maps	**OS Landranger 163; Explorer 169**
How to get there	**Arrive along B4696, the Spine Road, from the junction on the A419 4 miles south east of Cirencester**
Distance	**6 miles**
Time	**3 hours or more, depending on frequency of stops to look at the wild life**
Terrain	**Flat, easy walking, but may be muddy in places**
Refreshments	**Coots Café at the Gateway Centre close to the junction of A419 and B4696; Bakers Arms in the village (phone 01285 861298)**
Nearest TIC	**Cirencester (01285 654180)**

Cotswold Water Park extends over an area of 40 square miles and contains more than 140 lakes created by gravel extraction for over 50 years. The number of lakes keeps changing. It is an unusual area for the Cotswolds but the underlying geology of typical Cotswold stone is revealed in the buildings. On top of the oolitic limestone thick deposits of sand and gravel were laid down at the end of the Ice Age, carried by the melt water. It is these deposits which have been quarried and the holes filled with water to create the lakes, which are now used for a variety of activities. There is something for everyone, with centres for water sports, boating, sailing, water sking, wind surfing, as well as fishing, bird watching, miles of footpaths for walking. There are several picnic sites and there is even a beach. Several lakes are special for their bird life and hides have been constructed in many places. Nature Reserves have been developed in several locations but everywhere birds, flowers, insects and plants are an attraction throughout the year. Otters have been seen in the area, and beavers have been successfully reintroduced. Seasonal specialities include dragon flies in summer as well as migrant birds, but the winter visiting birds, ducks, geese, gulls and waders are even more numerous. Cotswold Water Park Society was created in 1996 as a non profit making organisation, which aims to look after wildlife as well as visitors (Office phone for fuller information 01793 752413).

Somerford Keynes is a Cotswold stone village with many fine houses, most notable being the Manor House adjacent to the church. The central part of the Manor probably dates from 15th and 16th century, with the east end being slightly later and with modern additions on the north west side. The church of All Saints is very old and, in 1985, the Parish celebrated 1300 years of Christianity on this site. Just inside the door on the left is a fragment of late Saxon sculpture which was probably part of a standing headstone to a grave. Straight across the nave on the north side is an Anglo Saxon doorway which may be the remains of a 7th century church. Also in the north aisle is the sculpture of a reclining figure, Robert Strange, who died in 1654. Other interesting features include the stone coffin lids set in the floor close to the font. The unusual font has a Norman bowl, standing on a 14th century hexagonal base. The church was restored in 1875.

The walk

1. Close to Somerford Keynes is the Neigh Bridge Country Park, with a large parking area. Walk back to the main road and turn left - signed Thames Path. After 200 yards turn right along a narrow road, signed to Lower Mill Estate - a new development of luxury second homes, which is still steadily expanding. On the left is Mill Lake (number 44), with a good information board. Pass new houses on the right. The road deteriorates to a track. At a gate with a Private Notice we turn right over a stream - the River Thames - and follow the clear path. Pass between two lakes and enjoy the view to the right where new housing development can be seen on the far side of the lake (number 57). Just before a metal gate we leave the Thames path and turn right, over a

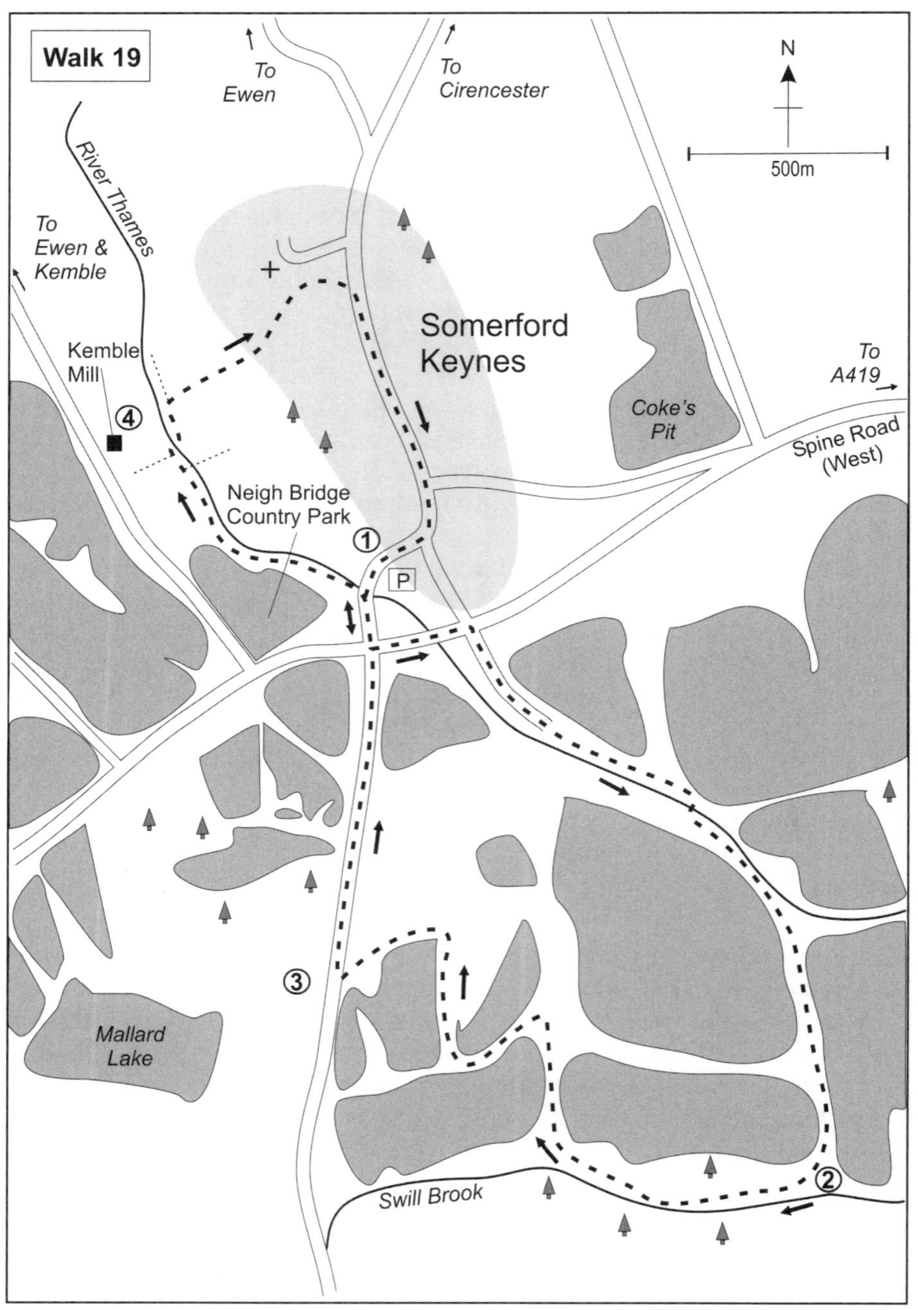
Walk 19
To Ewen
To Cirencester
N
500m
River Thames
To Ewen & Kemble
Somerford Keynes
To A419
Kemble Mill
④
Coke's Pit
Spine Road (West)
Neigh Bridge Country Park
①
P
③
Mallard Lake
Swill Brook
②

stile, and then walk along the left side of lake 41, passing another useful information board (Freeth Mere).

2. Beyond the end of the lake, at Pike Corner, with another information board, we turn right and keep straight ahead along the grassy path. When we reach the corner of this large meadow, cross the bridge (Otter Bridge) over Swill Brook. Walk ahead along Otter Corridor and the path divides. The right option leads alongside a fenced area, where beavers have been released, but we keep ahead along a large grass and wild flower meadow, with hedges and trees 30-40 yards away, both to the left and the right. Continuing along the large grassy area, some of which has been used for a rugby pitch, we come alongside a lake (58), and reach an information board which mentions the Flagham Fen Beaver project. The beavers seem to be thriving in what is a very suitable environment for them. We are now on a gravel track running alongside the lake, but to the left of this track is a signed footpath, which we must follow, and this takes us round the left side of a massive new housing development.

Views of the lakes

3. This winding path leads past the backs of the houses and keeps going between hedges and areas of undergrowth - yet more wonderful areas for wild life. We are passing the Swillbrook Lakes (numbers 46-48), a wonderful area for birds. We reach the road, where there is a board with information about the Swillbrook Lakes Nature Reserve we have just been walking through. Turn right along the road for a few hundred yards to reach the main road, and cross over to the Neigh Bridge Country Park (Point 1 again).

   Continue the walk from just beyond the entrance to the car park, following the Thames Path sign. Pass between the lake on our left (56) and the infant Thames. Reach a footbridge across the river and go on over here and through a modern metal gate on the far side of the bridge. Turn left to walk alongside the river.

4. At the end of the field, a path turns right but we keep ahead through a wooden kissing gate. Less than half way through this next, very large field, turn right across the field - there is a sign post in the hedge on our left. Cross this field to a footbridge and straight on across the next parkland type of field, with dovecot shaped building, the magnificent Manor House and then the church - all to our left. Ahead and to the right is Somerford House, with its gardens separated from the parkland by a ha-ha. Reach a kissing gate and to our left is a gate and stone stile leading into the churchyard, but our onward route is to the right, along the driveway. Keep straight ahead alongside a huge dry stone wall, passing the gate into Somerford House. On the left as we reach the road is the impressive Dower House with its clock just visible inside the courtyard. At the road, turn right to walk through the village, passing the smart stone buildings and colourful gardens, and the welcoming Bakers Arms. Straight on beyond there the road leads us back to our starting point in Neigh Bridge Country Park.

Not to be missed

Cotswold Country Park, formerly known as the Keynes Country Park. There is an admission charge, but ample parking and numerous attractions for all ages. The beach area is suitable for swimming and paddling and pedal boats are available for hire. The Watermark Café and Bar, exciting Head-4-Heights and play area are other attractions. Plus picnic and barbecue sites and footpaths for walks all around the lakes.

Source of the Thames

The source of the Thames is at Thames Head (grid reference 980994) near Kemble, and the river flows for 215 miles (346 km), the longest river which is entirely in England. The source can be reached by walking upstream along the Thames Path, from Ewen or Kemble, or a shorter walk from the Thames Head Inn (phone 01285 770259) on the A433 between Cirencester and Tetbury. Customers may leave cars here, with permission, and a walk of less than a mile will lead to the source – though the spring at the source is often dry is summer, when the river begins just north of Kemble. From the pub walk along the road (no footpath and speedy traffic, so be very careful) and just before the railway bridge turn left, following the footpath sign. After 200 yards alongside the railway line go over the stile, cross the railway and go over another stile, then walk diagonally across the field to a stile and gate. Go over the stile and turn right alongside the field margin for 100 yards to a signpost by a cattle drinking trough. Here is the Thames Path and turn left to walk across this large field. At the far side of the field is a small stone circle showing the site of the spring and behind this is the granite stone with the inscription 'The conservation of the River Thames 1857-1974. This stone was placed here to mark the source of the River Thames'. A footpath sign points downstream telling us that the Thames Path extends for 184 miles (294km) to the Thames Barrier in London. Just beyond the stone is the old pre-Roman camp on which stands Trewsbury House.

There is a difference of opinion about exactly where the Thames does rise, and many say that the real source is at Seven Springs, which would add 14 miles to the length of the Thames, but these springs are generally accepted as being the source of the River Churn (see Walk number 9).

Walk 20
Westonbirt

A gentle stroll on the Cotswold plateau takes us across farmland, through the small village of Westonbirt, Parkland of Westonbirt School and straight through the middle of the Westonbirt Arboretum.

Starting point	Arboretum car park – grid reference 849898. The spacious grassy parking area is suitable for picnics – if required. Payment is required for parking and entry to the Arboretum (phone number 01666 880220)
Maps	OS Explorer 168; Landranger 173
How to get there	Along the A433 south west of Tetbury, the turning into the Arboretum is clearly signed
Distance	Nearly 5 miles
Time	2-3 hours – but can be followed by more time wandering around the Arboretum
Terrain	Very gentle and mostly fairly level, but there can be muddy patches
Refreshments	Restaurant and café in the Arboretum, and a very good choice in nearby Tetbury
Nearest TIC	Tetbury (01666 503552)

Westonbirt House was designed in neo-Elizabethan style and built for Robert Stayner Holford by the English architect Lewis Vulliamy (1791-1871) between 1864-74. Vulliamy was also the architect for the Snooty Fox Hotel in Tetbury, and houses on Westonbirt village street. Westonbirt House became a Girls School in 1928, and the gardens, which were originally designed by Robert Holford, are open to the public on certain days during the school holidays.

The Walk

1. From the café restaurant called Maples and the car parking area walk down the grassy slope into the valley. Do not go through the small gate leading into the woods which slope up on the other side of the valley, but turn left. Walk along the grassy path on the bottom of the valley – following a blue arrow for the public bridleway. Go through a gate, across a driveway and pass to the right of the Plant Centre. An old stone wall is on our right, and beyond this the woods are part of the Silk Wood Section of the Arboretum. Walk along a tree lined path, then pass a large open field on our right and reach a notice saying Welcome to Westonbirt, which is where we leave the Arboretum. Keep straight ahead to cross the A433. Walk along the narrow road to pass a cross roads and reach the houses of Westonbirt Village on our left, with the open field on our right. These delightful stone houses all have very attractive gardens, very colourful in spring and summer. The village was formerly nearer the church, but was moved in mid 19th century to this present location to create the space for the new grand house.

The Plant Centre

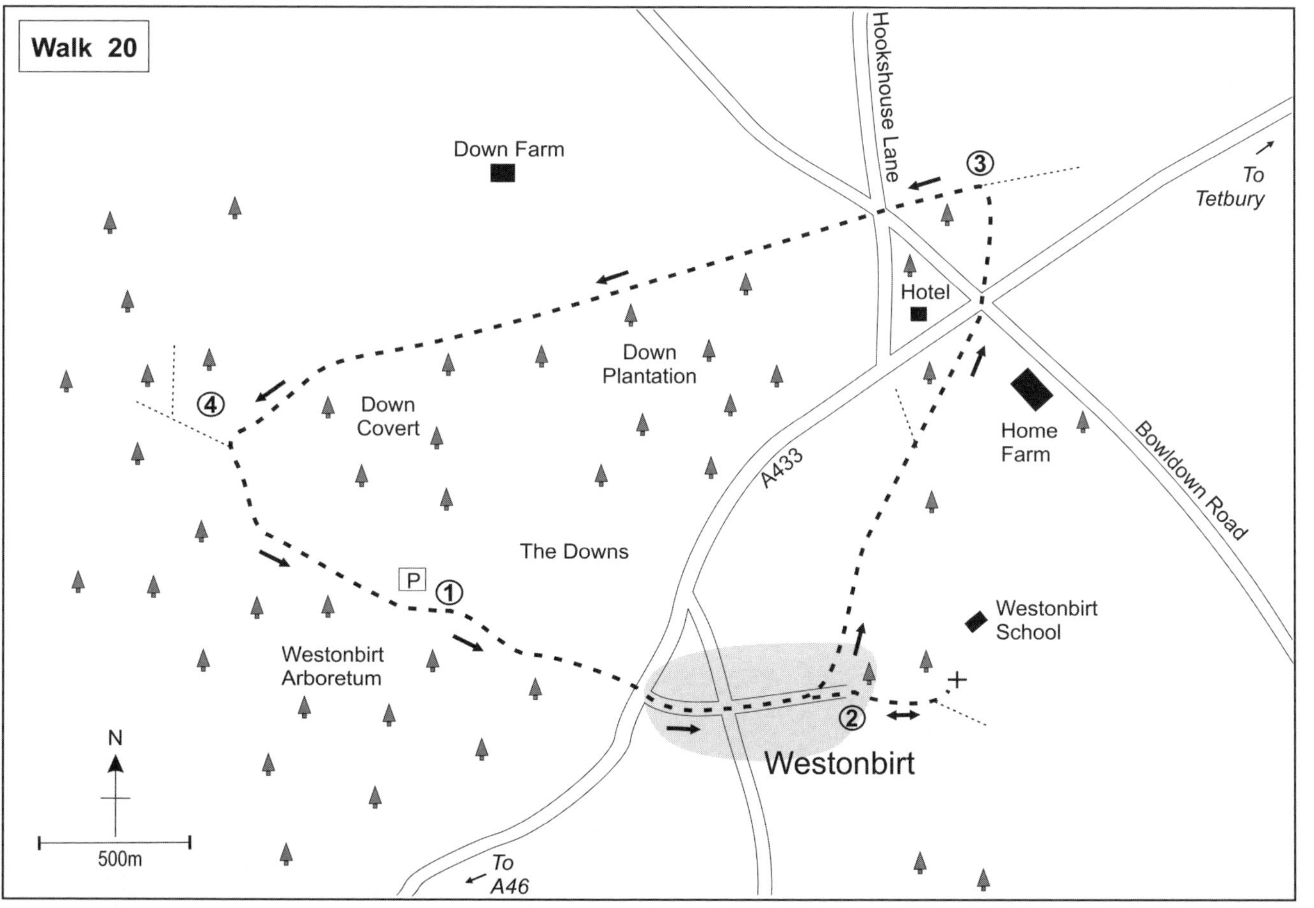
Walk 20
Down Farm
Hookshouse Lane
3
To Tetbury
Hotel
Down Plantation
4
Down Covert
Home Farm
A433
Bowldown Road
The Downs
P
1
Westonbirt School
Westonbirt Arboretum
2
Westonbirt
N
500m
To A46

Westonbirt House

At the end of the village is the driveway entrance to Westonbirt School and a public footpath which is our onward route, but first, keep straight ahead to the Golf Course and the church, where there is a car parking area - if required. To reach the church walk along the track which leads beneath a footbridge. The church of St Katharine may be locked, though it is now used as the chapel for Westonbirt School. Parts of the church date from the 14th century but much was restored in the 19th and early 20th centuries. The interior contains some interesting stained glass windows, an attractive font with octagonal bowl, and several memorials to the Holford family. Wonderful views from the churchyard reveal the magnificent Westonbirt House and also the gardens, which include Italian style terraces. The churchyard has many weathered grave stones including the tall memorial to Sir George Lindsay Holford (1860-1926).

2. Retrace steps from the church and turn right along the driveway into the park and to the school. The big house was built by Holford and

consists of three storeys but with a five storey tower. Used as a Girls School since 1928, it now has a Junior Department with boys and girls, but the main school is still all girls. Walk on through the park to reach a T-junction where the drive divides. Away to our left can be seen the lodge houses, to the right is the big house, but we keep straight ahead, along the grassy path, with a clump of trees to the right. Cross the next field, moving slightly away from the trees to our right, to reach a kissing gate in the fence, and continue across the middle of the next big field. Go on through a large metal gate and head towards the far left corner. Pass a magnificent large cedar tree and notice the Hare and Hounds Hotel on the main road to our left. At the cross roads, cross over to the footpath sign pointing into a clump of trees. Go on over the stile to walk along the right side of the three paddocks.

3. Reach a larger field and look for the large metal gate signed public bridleway, a few yards ahead on our left (and Monarch's Way), where we turn to walk past a house on the left and a few trees, with open field on the right. Keep ahead through a large wooden gate and along a broad grassy track to reach a cross roads. Keep straight ahead here, over the stile and along the right side of the large field, with a line of ash trees and a wall to our right, along what must have been a surfaced track sometime in the past. To our right here are the fields regularly used for polo, by the Beaufort Polo Club, from April until September. Reach a stile and a large gate, and keep straight on, with the fence now to our left. Go on over a stile, and the woods to our left are part of the arboretum, and through the trees can be seen open glades and rides in the old part of the Arboretum. For about half a mile just keep straight ahead over stiles, some of which are awkward asymmetric shapes, and pass through large fields, with views over to the right to the buildings of Down Farm. As we reach two smaller fields, notice there are trees straight ahead, down in the valley, but before reaching these trees, a large gate on the left is our route to re-enter the Arboretum, passing another Welcome to Westonbirt Arboretum notice.

4. We turn in through the gate and then walk downhill close to the right side of the field. At the bottom of the slope bend to the left to walk along the valley floor. The trees on our right are part of the Silk Wood section of the Arboretum. Reach a surfaced driveway, but cross over and keep on the path close to the fence – and the blue sign for Public bridleway. An area of silver trees on our right, includes the Common

Sea-Buckthorn, part of the Trail of Native Trees, one of many attractions in the Arboretum. Stay on the valley floor until reaching our starting point where we turn left to walk up the slope to the car parking area and also to Maples Restaurant, with its green roof, the Café, Forest Shop and Information Centre.

Tree bark with linear pattern

Not to be missed

After a pleasant walk around the glorious Cotswold landscape, spend a little time strolling around the Arboretum. The origins of Westonbirt can be traced back to Robert Stayner Holford who inherited Westonbirt in 1839. For anyone owning a fine country estate, collecting exotic plants was the fashion of the day. The arboretum was really created for his own enjoyment and he steadily collected and planted more trees. From 1880 Sir George Holford, Robert's son, took over the development of the Arboretum, and continued planting until his death in 1926. Now the National Arboretum and in the care of the Forestry Commission, it covers an area of 240 hectares (600 acres) and contains 16000 numbered trees and shrubs, from more than 3000 different varieties. Well worth visiting at any time of year, the Arboretum is particularly noted for the autumnal colours

Huge leaves of magnolia

but also for the displays of rhododendrons, azaleas and magnolias in spring, as well as the native wild flowers in the Silk Wood.

The rich variety of trees grown here is helped by the local geology. Situated at nearly 400 feet above sea level (120 metres), on the Jurassic limestone rocks which make up the Cotswolds, the soils are largely alkaline. But in several places there are acidic patches in surface layers, resulting perhaps from Ice Age deposits or from sandy loams dug up by badgers and rabbits. Also the arboretum creates its own micro climate and ecosystems, providing shelter in places and creating different conditions from those on the surrounding plateau area.

The free map available at the point of entry shows the two main sections of the Arboretum. The Old Arboretum is the area to the east of the car park, and the Silk Wood is to the west, on the other side of the valley which we walked along. The Old arboretum dates from the 1850s and contains rare and exotic trees as well as commoner varieties, but is laid out, with vistas - and can provide a short walk just wandering round the clear paths. It surrounds the open grassy area - The Downs.

Silk Wood also contains many varied and exotic trees but contains what was a working woodland dating back to the 13th century and is a quiet and more secluded area than the old Arboretum - and provides a longer walk if required. It is a semi natural woodland and is very ancient, having existed since the retreat of the last ice age about 12000 years ago.

Also from Sigma Leisure:

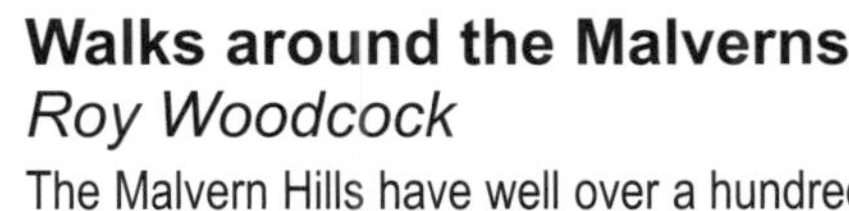

Walks around the Malverns

Roy Woodcock

The Malvern Hills have well over a hundred miles of paths on the hills and commons, and there is almost unlimited walking with real freedom to roam over many hectares of countryside. The hills are magnificent and the ridge walk is one of the finest in the country, with views east and west over large areas of rural England and into Wales. The 25 walks were selected to cover the entire range of hills and the adjacent commons; and, as the views looking at the hills can be as impressive as those looking from the hills, a few walks in the Ledbury area to the west and the Upton area and Old Hills to the east have been included.

£8.99

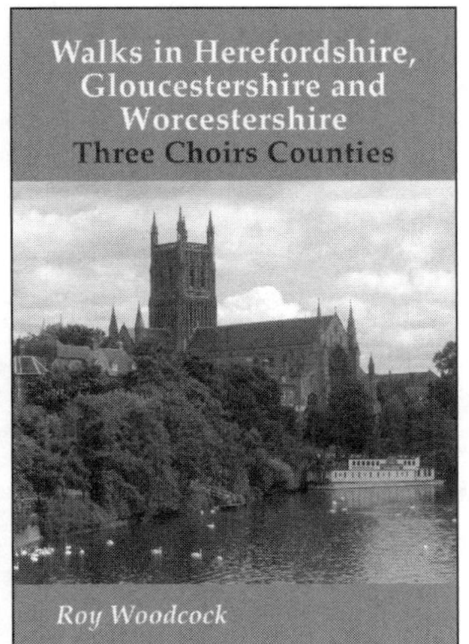

Walks in Herefordshire, Gloucestershire and Worcestershire

Three Choirs Counties

Roy Woodcock

The choice of walks takes ten locations from each of the Three Counties with routes through each of the three county towns, and across many of the best known landscapes as well as visiting several less well known areas. The walks are deliberately fairly short, from four to seven miles, which can be completed in half a day. Not strenuous or rugged, the walks are suited to anyone seeking a day out in the fresh air, with gentle exercise, whilst enjoying the beautiful views and countryside.

£8.99

Walking in the Cotswolds with children

Dave Meredith

Walking in the Cotswold with children is a book for parents whose children may not be as keen to go walking as they are. The Cotswolds offers some idyllic walking country and is Britain's largest officially designated 'Area of Outstanding Natural Beauty'. This book takes you to all the best places plus a few gems that even the locals aren't aware of. Paths follow well established rights-of-way and directions are clear enough for an older child to join in the fun by leading the walk. Along the way there are leaves to collect, questions to answer, tick lists and text of interest to children.

£8.99

Walks in the Forest of Dean and Wye Valley

Dave Meredith

The Forest of Dean and Wye Valley is a paradise for both the keen rambler and the casual stroller. The 22 walks described in this book are along easy footpaths taking you to spectacular viewpoints, along woodland glades carpeted with bluebells, daffodils and foxgloves, and under the dappled shade of its golden autumn canopy.

£8.99

Walks in the Midlands Countryside around Birmingham and the Black Country

Brian Conduit

In 1865 Elihu Burritt, a notable American peace and anti-slavery activist, was appointed the United States consul in Birmingham, at the time a rapidly growing manufacturing city and centre of a major industrial area. He travelling extensively throughout the Midlands. Burritt was full of enthusiasm for everything he saw and his obvious love for the area shines through in the book that he subsequently wrote about his journeys. That book, published in 1868, was entitled Walks in the Black Country and its Green Borderland. These 20 walks take you through areas of the Midlands which, 150 years since Burritt walked this way, still contain some of the most varied, beautiful and interesting landscapes and some of the finest old towns and villages in the country.

£8.99

Country Walks in and around Warwickshire

Ron Weston

This selection of 32 Warwickshire walks takes you on a journey of picturesque villages and historic churches, stately homes and castles, famous gardens and medieval tracks bound together by a superb network of public footpaths and canal towpaths and sometimes spilling over into adjoining counties. All walks in the book are circular, the longest being $5\frac{1}{2}$ miles and all within a radius of 25 miles from Coventry, with directions of how to get there and where to park.

£8.99

Heart of England Way
102 miles of linear walk or 225 miles of 32 linked circular walks

Stephen P Cross

A book both for the long distance and the leisure walker, The Heart of England Way, and 32 circular walks, takes the walker on a journey slicing through the quieter areas of midland, shire, countryside; from the north edge of Cannock Chase, to Bourton on the Water; providing a fascinating view through the back door of the regions history, people, buildings and landscape.

£8.99

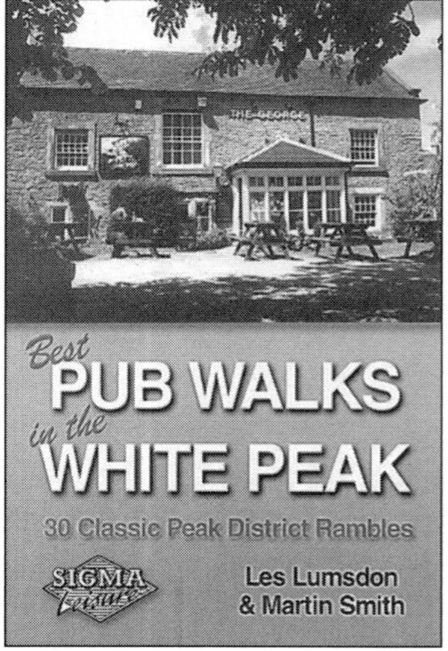

Best Pub Walks in the White Peak
30 Classic Peak District Rambles

Les Lumsden & Martin Smith

The 30 fabulous walks range from three to nine miles and ideal for family rambles. They start in such delightful Peak District villages as Ashford-in-the-Water, Alstonefield and Youlgreave, most of which are accessible by public transport — so that you can leave the car at home and savour the products on offer at the authors' favourite pubs.

Follow the recommendations in this well-established — and completely updated — book for a superb variety of walks in splendid scenery and, after each walk, relax in a Peak District pub renowned for its welcome to walkers and for the quality of its Real Ale, often supplied by local independent brewers.

£8.99

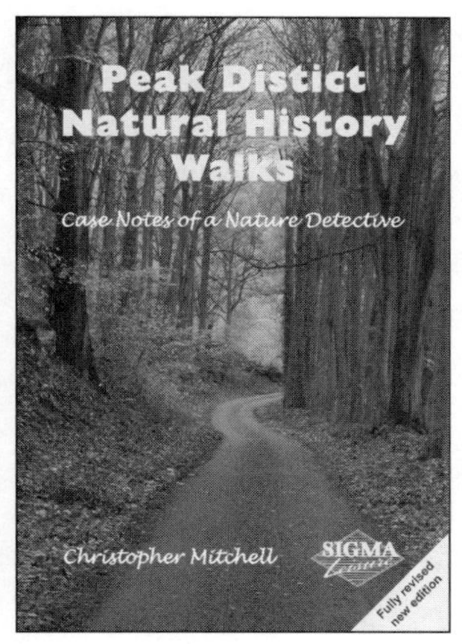

Peak District Walking Natural History Walks

Christopher Mitchell

An updated 2nd Edition with 18 varied walks for all lovers of the great outdoors — and armchair ramblers too! Learn how to be a nature detective, a 'case notes' approach shows you what clues to look for and how to solve them. Detailed maps include animal tracks and signs, landscape features and everything you need for the perfect natural history walk. There are mysteries and puzzles to solve to add more fun for family walks — solutions supplied! Includes follow on material with an extensive Bibliography and 'Taking it Further' sections.

£8.99

Best Tea Shop Walks in the Peak District

Norman and June Buckley

A wonderful collection of easy-going walks that are ideal for families and all those who appreciate fine scenery with a touch of decadence in the shape of an afternoon tea or morning coffee —or both! The 26 walks are spread widely across the Peak District, including Lyme Park, Castleton, Miller's Dale, and The Roaches and — of course — such famous dales as Lathkill and Dovedale. Each walk has a handy summary so that you can choose the walks that are ideally suited to the interests and abilities of your party. The tea shops are just as diverse, ranging from the splendour of Chatsworth House to more basic locations. Each one welcomes ramblers and there is always a good choice of tempting goodies.

£8.99

All-Terrain Pushchair Walks

Cheshire

Norman Buckley

30 graded walks, from level routes around pretty Cheshire villages to more adventurous hikes across the hillsides. Detailed directions and a map are provided for each route, together with some stunning photographs.

£8.99

Best Tea Shop Walks in Cheshire

Clive Price

"... A winning blend of scenic strolls and tasty tea shops." – Cheshire Life.

First published in August 1995 and sub-sequently updated with major revisions due to some tea shop closures and consequent re-routing of walks.

£8.99

Best Pub Walks in Cheshire 2nd Edition

Jen Darling

This is the second edition of a guidebook to the walks and pubs of Cheshire.

"I was delighted to be asked to put a few words on paper ... this book brings together a series of suggestions for your enjoyment." – John Ellis, Cheshire Tourism

£8.99

All of our books are available through booksellers.
For a free catalogue, please contact:

Sigma Leisure, Stobart House, Pontyclerc
Penybanc Road, Ammanford SA18 3HP

Tel: 01269 593100 Fax: 01269 596116

info@sigmapress.co.uk **www.sigmapress.co.uk**